# INTELLECTUAL PROPERTY ISSUES IN SOFTWARE

Steering Committee for Intellectual Property Issues in Software
Computer Science and Telecommunications Board
Commission on Physical Sciences, Mathematics, and Applications
National Research Council

National Academy Press
Washington, D.C. 1991

Support for this project was provided by the following organizations and agencies: Air Force Office of Scientific Research (Grant No. N00014-87-J-1110), Apple Computer, Inc., Control Data Corporation, Cray Research, Inc., the Defense Advanced Research Projects Agency (Grant No. N00014-87-J-1110), Digital Equipment Corporation, IBM Corporation, the National Aeronautics and Space Administration (Grant No. CDA-860535), the National Science Foundation (Grant No. CDA-860535), and the Office of Naval Research (Grant No. N00014-87-J-1110).

Library of Congress Catalog Card Number 90-62783
International Standard Book Number 0-309-04344-1

Available for sale from:
National Academy Press
2101 Constitution Avenue, NW
Washington, DC 20418
S227
Printed in the United States of America

# Preface

Computer software is a remarkable human achievement—whether measured by its extraordinary power to orchestrate computer hardware to carry out useful tasks; the creativity, talent, and teamwork required for its creation; the rapidity with which it is advancing technically; or the phenomenal growth of software as an economic activity. Nothing in human experience with technology is quite like it.

Twenty-five years ago sales of computer programs in the United States totaled an estimated $250 million. Today several thousand U.S. software producers—ranging from individuals to highly organized teams of hundreds or even thousands of computer scientists, software engineers, and programmers—generate revenues in the tens of billions of dollars. The systems and the application software they produce enable computers to support an ever-growing number of human activities.

In the early years of the Information Age, advances in computer and communications hardware drove progress in the computer-communications industry. Today it is software that adapts the hardware to the infinite range of human uses that gives the computer its personality and exploits its power. The manufacturers of computer hardware and software still gain a majority of their revenue from the hardware, but when the software created by users is included, people spend more on software than on hardware. For vertically integrated firms like IBM, software is, on the average, more profitable, and revenue from software is growing faster than revenue from hardware, in spite of the fact that proven software functions are continuously integrated into new hardware designs, and software designers move on to tackle yet newer tasks.

Thus the software industry is the enabling "complementary asset" for the hardware industry; those who master the challenge of creating good software can expect to be the leaders in the world of information machines and services. No one is prepared to predict that the extraordinary rate of growth and change is about to stop, or even slow down substantially. Both new applications and new computer architecture will continue to change the way we work, create, learn, communicate, and play.

Why then are computer scientists and software entrepreneurs nervous about the court decisions that guide the arcane legal world of intellectual property protection? And why do some intellectual property lawyers become even more nervous when scientists question the rationale underlying the current structure of legal protection and even suggest that it may be inadequate or cause serious problems in the future?

The world of software has changed dramatically since the emergence of commercial software in the 1950s. Initially the work of mathematicians and scientists who were intimately involved in building computer hardware, software was the creative expression of gifted individuals. With IBM's decision to "unbundle" software—pricing it separately from the hardware—and later the development of high-level design languages to lower the technical barriers to programming, the team approach to software production began to look much more like the modus operandi in the more traditional areas of commercial product design and testing.

Today in the largest firms, products comprising millions of lines of "code" are produced in industrial environments against committed plans for function, cost, and date of delivery. But even in these mature commercial environments, the role of the designer who is able to keep the conception of system-level design in mind, and who oversees the integration of hundreds of modules into a functioning whole, is still the key to product success. An evolving combination of intuition, prior experience, and expertise in computer and cognitive science go into the production of "user-friendly," efficient, error-free code.

But the institutional structure of the industry is maturing. There are large numbers of firms with market positions to protect, with customers dependent on the continuous, incremental improvement of their applications. The magnitude of the up-front investments required to create competitive software products, and of the downstream investments needed to sell and support them, inevitably gives rise to conflicting desires to encourage innovation while preserving stability in a huge, competitive industry.

The maturing of the industry is not the result of saturating growth but reflects instead the industry's success in becoming integrated into the fabric of modern society. End users want to assemble for their needs the best of the industry's output. They want familiar, reliable, and predictable ways to do things. They cannot sort through thousands of packages to find the best ones; they are demanding that the industry—through strategic alliances, standards development, or simply response to market forces—provide more interoperability, consistent interfaces, and very high levels of reliability.

Market entry for new innovators is still wide open, however, as far as industry structure, the legal environment, and emerging markets are concerned.

But the cost of entry is soaring; negotiating compatibility with other products, testing, advertising, and providing customer support and continuous product evolution as the hardware and software around the product change—all entail high risks and heavy up-front investment. No wonder those who spend millions of dollars to develop and bring to market products that cost virtually nothing to replicate or manufacture want assurances that they will have a chance to enjoy the fruits of their labors.

Three fears seem to be dominant in the minds of industry leaders:

- fear of loss of freedom of action,
- fear of litigation over possible infringement of patents and copyrights, and
- fear of unfair business practices that deny risk-takers the fruits of their creativity.

A fourth fear is voiced by the scientists and entrepreneurs entering the market:

- fear that business practices and legal constraints will slow down the process of shared learning on which future progress rests.

This is the very process that led the framers of the Constitution to enshrine copyright and patent law with constitutional authority. A fifth fear is less frequently voiced, perhaps because the public has been so well served by software innovators of the last 40 years, but nevertheless deserves consideration:

- fear that the public interest in software will be subordinated to the interests of the industry.

From a bystander's perspective, legal protection of software today may not seem very complicated, nor in serious difficulty. Relatively few software patents have been issued, and even fewer have been tested in court. Copyright protection is almost universally available, is inexpensive, and little constrains the entry of new firms or the growth of the industry. Contractual commitments by buyers to sellers are generally respected, especially in business environments.

Freedom of action has been the hallmark of the first 40 years; its attraction for innovators is the very factor that breeds fear of its loss. Larger computer hardware firms extensively cross-license their patents, preserving freedom to innovate in the hardware. To the extent that software copyright does not grant exclusivity to ideas or to function, but only to their expression, that freedom of action is preserved, for the software industry as well.

But for those inclined to worry about the future there are worries enough. At the practical level, software vendors are using multiple levels of protection: trade secret rights, copyright law, publishing only in hard-to-understand "object code," binding users by contract, and—increasingly—seeking patent protection as well. On the face of it, this defense-in-depth strategy seems to suggest that the firms are less than fully confident that the property protection system is robust.

A second concern arises from the tensions of stretching a system designed for works of art and literature to works of great value for their utility (as well as occasional intellectual elegance). Is a copyright violated by a product whose form and function emulate another's but whose code is never identical? Is it legitimate to use a reverse compiler to create source code from a copyrighted product shipped only in object code, and then recompile to a different machine a restructured version of the original? How will the notion of "copying" be applied when a user's inquiry for information from distributed databases in communications networks momentarily touches small parts of dozens of separately copyrighted programs? Lawyers are perhaps more comfortable with the need to stretch and adapt legal precedents to changes in technology than are scientists. This happens in every branch of the law. But many scientists and some legal scholars see the stretching of patent and copyright law to cover the rapidly changing field of software property as a source of discomfort, if not of serious concern.

The third concern is seen by some as a little black cloud on the horizon: the resurgence of patent filings on inventions primarily embodied in software. Some may see this trend as offering an alternative to the pressure to distort copyright law to protect the most creative elements of a program rather than just a boring sequence of hexadecimal numbers. But others ask, with the standards as yet unsettled for software "inventions," what costs will be added to the development process when software developers must ensure that the protected ideas of others have not been independently created by their staffs. They fear that software patents, if not strictly managed by the Patent and Trademark Office, will be a boon to litigators and a nightmare for software developers. Still others believe that with so many software inventions already in the public domain, few patents will withstand challenge, but the costs of challenging will be high. Perhaps these are just "growing pains" of a maturing industry, and the gains afforded by widespread use of software patents will more than make up for the costs. But perhaps not.

The fourth, and most important, concern is over the ability of the courts and the Congress to keep up with the pace of technical change. Although copyright has proved elastic enough to extend from maps and charts in the 18th century to books, works of art, movies, and audio and video tapes, none of these technologies has exhibited the pace of change of software. When computer scientists and entrepreneurs try to understand the rationales used by judges to adapt the law to technical change, they get more nervous still. Many cases whose resolution strikes the layman as fair and judicious are explained in opinions that describe the technology (often by analogy) in ways the scientists cannot easily accept. That judges may not think like computer scientists does not mean they make bad law. But it may amplify the concerns of technical people trying to guess where the law is going next. And it motivates legal scholars to try to understand the industry's technical destiny as the reference frame for evaluating the legal structure on which future decisions will rest.

That lawyers and scientists approach this subject differently will surprise no one. Technical people set their sights on the future, probing the limits of today's technology and laying the groundwork for tomorrow's innovations. Change, surprise, even disruption are not the enemies of science, but rather its purpose. The law values coherence with the past, predictability, and a broad consensus. Judges and attorneys build on precedent to deal with questions arising from new technology. In so doing they build an architecture of reasoning on which the framework for resolving future issues must rest. Scientists, engineers, and software designers sometimes question the appropriateness of that architecture for what they see coming in the technology.

It is not just legal and technical experts who sometimes have differing views. The perspectives of academic computer scientists sometimes differ from those of software entrepreneurs; legal scholars tend to be more critical of the existing protection regime than do the litigators and corporate counsel.

## NATURE OF THIS PROJECT

Would a wide-ranging discussion between computer and legal experts help to clarify the basic issues that set directions for the future in the field of intellectual property protection for software?

That is the basic question that motivated a workshop held on September 12-13, 1989 (Appendix A), and a forum discussion in December 1989 (Appendix B) sponsored by the Computer Science and Technology Board (since renamed the Computer Science and Telecommunications Board) of the National Research Council. About 100 legal scholars, attorneys, computer scientists, software designers and entrepreneurs, and business and government executives aired the views that are summarized (with updates as appropriate) in this report.

The forum discussion did not seek to find a consensus, nor did it entertain collective recommendations. Rather, the goal was to foster a common understanding among individuals and groups who have a stake in the issues but who have had few opportunities to share their points of view. The discussion did not seek to deal with current controversies, and certainly not with current litigation. Instead the forum sought to take a step back from the debate and explore basic concepts—both technical and legal—that are too often obscured by polemics.

The success of the forum, and of the two-day workshop that preceded it, lies in the often expressed view at the end of the meetings that a number of important issues explored there deserved to be engaged by a mixed group of legal and technical experts in much greater depth. This reflection of confidence that differing perceptions could be bridged provides a basis for considerable optimism about the value of this kind of exchange.

## ORGANIZATION OF THE REPORT

This publication is based primarily on discussions at the two-day forum and at the preceding two-day planning workshop attended by many of the speakers at the forum. It also draws on articles and reports distributed to forum and workshop participants, as well as on other informational materials. These additional sources are identified within the text.

The following chapters describe the spectrum of legal and technical perspectives on intellectual property protection for software. Chapter 1 discusses some of the changing technical, economic, and legal circumstances that underlie the debate over the adequacy of intellectual property protection for software. In chapter 2, the underlying tenets of U.S. copyright, patent, and trade secret laws are described, as are issues that have arisen in the application of these laws to software. Chapter 2 also discusses international treatment of software as intellectual property. The attributes of software, the nature of the process for designing and developing software, and the relevance of both to determining which elements of software merit protection are examined in chapter 3. Chapter 4 takes a closer look at legal uncertainties, how software firms are responding to these uncertainties, and how intellectual property protection can influence standardization, including ongoing efforts to increase the interoperability of software applications. The final chapter, Chapter 5, presents some forum participants' views on how to improve the fit between software and intellectual property law.

The primary authors of this report are C.K. Gunsalus, associate vice chancellor for research at the University of Illinois at Urbana-Champaign and consultant to the Computer Science and Telecommunications Board (CSTB), and Mark Bello, also a consultant to the CSTB. The project was organized by C.K. Gunsalus in conjunction with Marjory Blumenthal, CSTB staff director. Their authorship was performed under the supervision of the steering committee, which was responsible for the conduct of the workshop and the forum and which expresses its deep appreciation for the work of the staff and consultants. While the authors and the steering committee members have done their best to make this account faithful to the views expressed at the meeting and in other sources, we request that readers not use this document to attribute the views of forum participants who are quoted. Please contact them directly for full and in-context accounts of their views.

Lewis M. Branscomb, *Chairman*
Steering Committee for Intellectual Property
Issues in Software

# Contents

1 **Changing Contexts for the Software Industry**     3
    A Maturing Industry, 6
    Changing Technology, 9
    Changing Legal Context, 12
    Unpredictable Future, 14
    Conclusion, 16
    Notes, 18

2 **Background to Basic Legal Issues**     21
    Copyright, 22
       Expressions, Ideas, and Functions, 24
       What Constitutes Copyright Infringement?, 27
    Trade Secret, 29
    Patent, 31
       Characteristics of Patents, 32
       What Is Patentable?, 34
          Test for Patentability, 35
          Coherent or Incoherent?, 37
    The International Situation, 38
    Notes, 41

3 **Is Software a Special Case?**     43
    The Process, 43
    Software as a Creative Medium, 48
    The Influence of the Market, 49

Symbiosis in the Market, 50
The Case of Interfaces, 51
    Evolution of User Interfaces, 54
    Where Does Innovation Lie?, 55
Summary, 57
Note, 57


**4  A Closer Look at Current Issues**                               **59**
Protected or Unprotected?, 60
The Patent-Copyright Interface, 62
Patent Problems:  Structural or Legal?, 63
Compatibility and Interoperability, 66
    Open Interfaces, a Controversial Suggestion, 68
    Immediate Declaration of Rights, 69
    Standardization, 70
The Influence of Intellectual Property Law, 73
Withholding of Source Code, 75
Reverse Engineering, 77
Conclusion, 78
Notes, 79


**5  The Open Agenda**                                               **81**
Defining a Concept of Value, 83
Legislative "Solutions"?, 84
Hybrid System for Hybrid Technologies?, 87
Incremental Improvements to Patent System?, 89
Next Steps, 90
Notes, 93


**6  Bibliography**                                                  **95**


**Appendix A**   Intellectual Property Challenges in Software—
                 Workshop Program and Participants, 101


**Appendix B**   Intellectual Property Issues in Software—
                 Forum Program and Participants, 107

# INTELLECTUAL PROPERTY ISSUES IN SOFTWARE

The question is whether, as to copyright protection for computer software, "the sky is falling." . . . I submit, "It just ain't so."
—Morton David Goldberg, *Partner, Schwab, Goldberg, Price, & Dannay*

[M]y answer to that is, the truth is the sky is falling all around you. It just hasn't hit you yet.
—Jerome H. Reichman, *Professor of Law, Vanderbilt University*

I don't think the sky is falling. I think it is sagging in a few places, and primarily because the law hasn't been properly applied.
—Ronald S. Laurie, *Partner, Irell & Manella*

Market-mediated innovation is definitely the way to go, and my bottom line on the intellectual property front is let us not screw it up. The agonizing thing is, I cannot tell whether that means do nothing or do something radical.
—Mitchell D. Kapor, *Chairman, ON Technology, Inc.*

I thought of concluding today with the adage, "If it ain't broke, don't fix it." But that does not truly reflect my views, which are stronger than that. So, I will conclude with a new adage, "If it ain't broke, don't break it."
—Howard G. Figueroa, *Vice President, Commercial and Industry Relations, IBM Corp.*

# 1

# Changing Contexts for the Software Industry

An idea and a computer. Those two items, it has often been said, are all that is needed to enter the software industry. Although this characterization fails to convey the enormous range in the size of software firms, as well as in the complexity of computer programs and the underlying design and development efforts, it is accurate insofar as it captures the industry's vitality and its propensity for innovation.

Indeed, the software industry possesses all the attributes of a vigorous economic sector: stiff competition, a diverse mixture of firms, rapid sales growth, high rates of commercial innovation, strong performance in international markets, and, as the "idea and a computer" adage suggests, low barriers to entry. Market statistics vary, but they suggest that over the past twenty-five years the number of U.S. software firms has quadrupled, and the size of the product market has been doubling about every five years. In 1990, sales of packaged software alone by U.S. software firms totaled nearly $20 billion and accounted for more than 40 percent of the world market (International Data Corporation estimate cited in U.S. Department of Commerce, 1991); U.S. purchases of "software products" (excluding custom-developed software) amounted to $35 billion in 1990 according to another estimate (personal communication, INPUT, March 6, 1991).

Given this enviable track record and the outlook for continued rapid sales growth, it would seem that the industry faces a bright future. But some see the path to that future obstructed by uncertainty over intellectual property protection for software and by the adversarial behavior that has arisen in this climate of uncertainty. The result, said Robert Spinrad, director of corporate technology at Xerox Corp., is confusion, which is having a "stultifying, dulling effect" and "slowing down the activity" of firms big and small.

There are clear signs that legal concerns have become matters of paramount importance in an industry that, for most of its history, was unfettered by such concerns. One sign is the recent spate of copyright- and patent-infringement cases, in which firms are charging that the commercial fruits of their innovative efforts have been unfairly usurped by others. Another is the flurry of filings for patents on software-related innovations. Until only a few years ago, it was widely believed that patents were largely unavailable for software. The result, according to critics of patent protection for software, is a fundamental change in the rules that have governed the behavior of software firms. A third sign is in evidence in Europe. There, software firms have divided into two camps and squared off over a European Commission proposal that would codify the application of copyright law to software (Verity, 1990).

Diagnoses of the current state of affairs vary widely, as do prognoses of how intellectual property concerns will affect the pace of innovation in software and the health of the industry. The quotations presented at the beginning of this chapter are representative of the diversity of opinion. Most notable about this spectrum of perspectives, perhaps, is not the viewpoints themselves, but rather the fact that in every quarter of software-related activity—business, government, and academia—people have strongly held opinions on what and how rights of ownership should be applied to software.

Until only recently, intellectual property concerns were limited almost entirely to piracy, or the direct copying of software. Independent software developers and firms had wide latitude of action, and many software inventions were believed to be in the public domain, available for all to use and to build upon. Some new software products—for example, the first database management systems, the first Fortran compiler, or the first timesharing operation system—represented major advances. Most, however, offered incremental improvements, such as support for new hardware models, adaptation to a new market niche, or greater ease of use.

This environment accommodated independent innovation, in which different developers created separate products to accomplish the same task. One need only peruse the variety of offerings for two of the most common software applications—word processing and spreadsheets—to find evidence of this phenomenon. The freewheeling atmosphere also fostered successive rounds of improvement in products with established markets. For a firm to be satisfied with the performance and functionality of an existing product was to risk losing market share to a competitor that targeted the same market niche. The nature of competition in the industry has been such that, if there is a perceived market for a particular software product, "someone will build it, and someone else will, as well," said Harry C. Reinstein, chairman and chief executive officer of the Aion Corp.

While many software firms were aware of what intellectual property protection applied to software—primarily trade secret law and copyright law—the actions of most firms suggested that legal concerns rarely entered into product-development decisions. The collective behavior of firms served to achieve the constitutional aim on which intellectual property law is based: "to promote the progress of science and the useful arts." More specifically, the software industry achieved the intent of intellectual property law, that is, to advance the public good, an objective widely interpreted to mean the generation and wide dissemination of ideas and innovations.

Today's legal ferment indicates that software firms are much more attuned to intellectual property issues. And why not? Copyright law and patent law exist to encourage innovation. Both award limited monopolies to those who invest their resources, effort, and ingenuity in developing products that society may deem useful. Thus intellectual property law offers the potential for private financial gain as an incentive for undertaking the risks of innovation.

To Francis D. Fisher, adviser to the Educational Technology Group at the Harvard Law School, concerns that innovation in software will diminish without strong intellectual property protection seem at odds with the industry's historically high rate of innovation. "It is not enough to suggest that the incentives of monopoly are needed," Fisher maintained. "We need evidence. We need to shift the burden of proof, so that those who believe that the public interest gains from extending property rights to software must prove their case." Among those who believe this case is unproven is Richard Stallman, whose Free Software Foundation and League for Programming Freedom provide a test of his conviction that innovation is best served absent prices based on commercial monopoly.[1]

While Fisher may be unconvinced of the need to accord strict intellectual property rights to software, the perception that software is vulnerable to abuses by competitors and users is widespread. Firms trying to position themselves in the market to earn returns on their investment often devote considerable thought to protection strategies. But in the end, said Peter R. Schneider, IBM Corp. vice president for systems and programming, "this is a crap shoot. . . . I cannot depend on my lawyers or the legal system" to identify a single measure that, on its own, will provide adequate protection. As a result, a firm may take advantage of all the available protections.[2] "[I]t is like there is a disease out there," Schneider explained, "and massive doses of mixed antibiotics are best, because I am not sure which one of them is going to be the silver bullet."

The uncertainty that Schneider expresses stems from doubts about the scope of intellectual property law and, in particular, how patent and copyright laws apply to the innovative elements embodied in a software product. "The current environment is such that you don't know the right thing to do," said Anita K. Jones, head of the University of Virginia Computer Science Department and co-founder of a small software firm. "So, you act in a very protective fashion."

Assertions like those made by Jones and Schneider raise two fundamental questions. Why do firms—even large ones with access to the best legal advice—perceive the need to act so protectively, and why are they unsure of the applicability of the 200-year-old body of intellectual property law to software? Some insight into these questions can be gained by examining the changing and often unpredictable economic, technical, legal, and social influences that are shaping the industry.

## A MATURING INDUSTRY

Software is big business, and if forecasts of continued rates of sales growth exceeding 10 percent are accurate, it will become a much bigger business during the next decade. Japan, the nations of Western Europe, and other countries have taken steps to foster the development of internationally competitive software industries. Not coincidentally, many of these nations are also wrestling with questions concerning intellectual property protection for software.

The economic importance of software has risen dramatically over the last three decades. During the 1960s, computer manufacturers provided little software beyond the operating system, which was necessary to the functioning of the machine. In the mid- to late-1960s, IBM began "unbundling" software from its hardware products, and other computer makers followed the example of the industry leader. In addition, the service bureaus of computer manufacturers and independent automated data processing firms were major sources of leased software, as were computer users who developed their own programs. The best of the user-developed software was marketed and supported by computer manufacturers.

These changes sowed the seeds of the software industry. In 1970 U.S. expenditures for software products totaled an estimated $500 million. That number grew to an estimated $1 billion in 1975 and approached $3 billion in 1980 (CBEMA, 1990). In succeeding years, as noted above, sales, the number of firms, and the number of software applications mushroomed.

At some point in the evolution of most industries, annual increases in sales begin to taper off, and product niches become crowded with competitors. In the software industry, the growing tide of litigation may mark the early stages of this maturation process, when firms devote less time to prospecting, begin to stake out their territories, and start prosecuting trespassers. The competitive landscape fills up.

Such a scenario is, of course, highly speculative. The general expectation is that innovation and new product development will proceed at a rapid clip. As Bruce Tognazzini, designer of dozens of programs for Apple Computer, Inc., said in regard to human interfaces, "You ain't seen nuthin' yet," and he reminded that "little companies are the major innovators out there, still." Tognazzini's outlook, with which many software industry analysts would concur, suggests that there is still much new territory for software firms to explore.

Nonetheless, the steadily growing number of software firms, both in the United States and abroad, means that the population of prospectors combing the terrain for new commercial opportunities is also increasing. Moreover, established firms have already made substantial investments in developing products and building a customer base for those products. For these firms, innovation can have some negative consequences. If an innovation by a competitor has the potential to supplant existing products, it jeopardizes the established firm's revenue stream and, thus, its return on past investments. And for the established firm to stay competitive, it will have to make new investments in research, development, and marketing. Even if the innovation is the established firm's own creation, it may not translate into substantial new revenue growth. Rather, it may help the firm maintain its customer base and avert a loss in sales.

Start-up firms, in contrast, are not constrained by past investments, nor must they worry about carving up an existing customer base. In relative terms, start-up firms may realize greater returns on innovation than do firms with established product lines.

Compared with the early days of the software industry, explained Lewis M. Branscomb, director of the Science, Technology, and Public Policy Program at Harvard University's John F. Kennedy School of Government, "there are more stakeholders, and the stakeholders are generally more heavily invested than before. Large investments produce new inelasticities in the system. Technological changes create conflict because they are harder to accommodate."

To protect their investments and maintain their position in the market, firms will take advantage of whatever tools are available, including intellectual property law. Although the law is not intended to guarantee profits, ownership rights accorded through the law do provide innovators the opportunity to earn a return on their creative efforts in the market, the ultimate judge of the commercial value of a particular innovation.

Eliminate the financial incentive for making software, suggested John F. Shoch, general partner at the Asset Management Co., and today's intellectual property disputes would disappear, but so would the pipeline of products that add new capability after new capability to the computer. "If software had no value and nobody wanted to buy it, this would be a very academic discussion," Shoch maintained. "It would be a wonderful hobby. It wouldn't be a business, and nobody would care where intellectual property boundaries are drawn because no one would be making any money, and no one would bother filing a lawsuit."

Economic analyses provide support for Shoch's contention. Schumpeter, Scherer (1984), and other economists, Branscomb explained, have clearly shown that without some form of temporary protection for inventions, the market, by itself, "will not support the risks and costs of technical progress." This may be especially true for software, which can require large expenditures for development but costs virtually nothing to manufacture—or to copy.

Software's inherent vulnerability to copying seems to underscore the need for protection that encourages individuals and businesses to pursue new ideas and new computer applications, producing benefits for the larger society. But the prospect of private gain, intellectual property law's incentive for innovation, spawns vested interests and the inclination for firms to act according to their own needs, which may not coincide with the public's or even the industry's best interests. Thus there is also the inclination for firms to wield intellectual property protection as a tactical weapon against competitors.

There are some indications—and even more allegations—of such behavior in the software industry. In a recent law suit, one firm claimed that a competitor was "using its copyrights to hold the computer industry hostage by its licensing and litigation practices" (Pollack, 1990). At issue in several pending law suits is retroactive declaration of ownership rights. According to some industry observers, firms that initially promoted widespread use of particular innovations to cultivate the market for their own commercial implementations, later have declared the innovations proprietary and demanded royalties for their use.

Thus questions about the applicability of intellectual property protection to software must be considered in the context of how firms are likely to use the available protection to advance their position in the market.

## CHANGING TECHNOLOGY

As the power and speed of computers have increased, so have the utility, complexity, and, ultimately, the importance of software. Advances in hardware stimulate new rounds of software innovation, resulting in new applications that expand the role of software and move the computer toward its projected incarnation as the universal machine.

"In every new generation of hardware," Branscomb said, "function that was previously provided in software is often incorporated in the hardware, where it can be more efficiently executed. Nevertheless, as the technology evolves, new layers of software are developed, which bring new functions to the hardware, and this ever-growing bubble of capability seems not only to be adding new function, but an even larger fraction of the function is delivered through layers of software."

One consequence of this evolution is software's growing share of the expense associated with computer systems. Another is difficult questions about where value, or the intellectual property, lies in software and how best to protect those elements that surpass a certain threshold of creativity. While once proscriptions against outright copying of program code might have been accepted as sufficient means to address abuses that undermine intellectual property rights, today the concepts of value and sufficient creativity require clarification to guide the application of the law to issues that go well beyond the copying of code.

Although these concepts are subject to interpretation, a recognized criterion of value is the nature of the interaction between a software application and the user. "As time has moved on," explained Schneider of IBM, "more and more of the creative output has been focused on interfaces, and that is simply a reflection of the fact that in order to grow in our industry we are spending less energy figuring out how to do task dispatching and memory management and more energy focusing on how to interface with the end user and how to expand the marketplace."

The emphasis on developing software that mimics and complements the behavior of the human user makes ergonomic factors important determinants of value in software. Many in the industry believe that limiting intellectual property protection solely to the copying of code is an inadequate safeguard for the creativity, as well as the underlying financial investment, embodied in software that, in effect, meshes with the intuitions, needs, and predilections of the user. While charges of verbatim copying have not disappeared, software firms are now asking the courts to determine whether competitors copied the "look and feel" or "structure, sequence, and organization" of a software product, despite substantial differences in the code of the original and competing products. While all courts agree that a program's functionality is not copyrightable, courts disagree on the extent to which particular elements of a computer program constitute functional subject matter.

Interfaces, generally defined as the boundary between two environments, are critical to satisfying user demand for achieving the compatibility and interoperability of independent software applications. As the web of computers and related information technologies grows, the value and utility of software are largely defined by its role in some larger system—by its ability to interface and work with other applications. As a result, users are objecting to obstacles to interoperability imposed by the idiosyncrasies of proprietary system interfaces.

Computer manufacturers and software developers are responding to this demand, as the rapid growth of networking attests and the momentum for so-called open systems also grows. But, again, these technological changes are altering the identity of software and generating new questions, including how to price software.

Software applications, according to Esther Dyson, publisher of the software industry newsletter "Release 1.0," are evolving from discrete packages of functionality into collections of functions that users can invoke individually. "Software is going to be much more fluid," she said. "You won't know what computer it runs on. You are going to sit at a terminal and ask for a service. Where that service gets executed you probably won't know." And during the execution of that service, Dyson continued, functions performed by many different pieces of software—residing perhaps on many different machines—may participate in accomplishing a specific task. In essence carrying out a user request will create the software equivalent of "going to a prime contractor who uses a variety of subcontractors." Such fluidity and interoperability among software applications will undermine existing pricing systems. "If I use three pieces of software but only a small part of the functionality of each," Dyson asked, "whom do I pay? How do I get charged?"

The answers are not clear. "We are not at all sure we know how to control the assets"—software—once they are available in a distributed computing network, said Schneider of IBM. "The free flow through LANs [local area networks] says we have gotten to the point where we are not sure how to bill for software anymore." One potential pricing mechanism is an enterprise-wide contract, in which software suppliers receive a fraction of client revenues. If software pricing is troublesome, so too will be the allocation of royalties for its use.

Even more problematic are questions about the rights of ownership accorded to each of the application components that are combined and recombined to create a customized work of software at the user's behest. Today, questions about what constitutes fair use of software elements and what distinguishes a derivative work from an original one focus primarily on the behavior of designers and program implementors. Tomorrow, Dyson noted, users who create software as a byproduct of running a business (and potentially a product or source of competitive advantage) will become part of the conundrum.

In this fluid environment, the corollary to the question of what elements of software warrant protection becomes a critical issue. That is, if the goal of interoperability is to be fully realized, then the software industry will have to determine what elements should not be protected, and therefore freely licensed. For example, several forum participants advocated "open" program-to-program interfaces. Objectors to this proposal argued that the decision of whether to declare an interface proprietary or open should rest with the innovator. The popularity of a widely used interface should be incentive enough to make it generally available. However, software vendors want to be reassured that they do not lose the rights to the underlying code when they publish the interfaces, and users want reassurances that a royalty for the interface will not be imposed once its popularity is established and its use becomes a necessity.

Yet another technological development—automated reverse engineering technology—has the potential to complicate the application of intellectual property law to software. Already available technology can in certain circumstances decompile, or translate, computer code into a higher-level language, mechanically restructure the program, and generate new computer code that, by appearance, is substantially different from the original. Some forum participants minimized the potential for abuses posed by this technology, at least in its current form. Branscomb, for example, noted that the technology "works only on clean, well-structured object [machine-readable] code." The recompiled code, he added, "is still undocumented and will be very hard to maintain." But if abuses do arise, several legal experts pointed out, intellectual property law may not be an effective means of redress. If the copied version and the original are substantially dissimilar and there is no evidence of reverse compilation, they said, judges and juries will be hard pressed to find infringement.

## CHANGING LEGAL CONTEXT

The constitutional foundation of intellectual property law precedes by nearly two centuries the introduction of computers and software. Obviously, the framers of this body of law never anticipated computer software. Nor, however, did they foresee such developments as motion pictures, record albums, compact disks, and numerous other technologies and expressions now protected by copyright law. To some, the demonstrated flexibility of intellectual property law strongly indicates that the legal system can continue to adapt to new technologies and to handle questions related to software. Unlike most other technologies, however, software may be eligible for both patent and copyright protection, which introduces a significant source of uncertainty.

"[P]atent and copyright law have survived as long as they have survived," maintained Frank Ingari, head of marketing and development in the Spreadsheet Division of Lotus Development Corp., "because they have shown a remarkable capability to deal with wave upon wave of technology and wave upon wave of innovation and industrial development."

Those who are confident in the providence of the legal system see today's intellectual property disputes as the consequence of an inevitable gap between the rate of technological progress and the pace of the law. Confusion and uncertainty will diminish, according to this view, as courts resolve today's issues. Ideally, the decisions will yield predictable rules for firms to follow and guideposts for addressing unforeseen issues that are certain to arise with new developments in the rapidly changing field.

Computer scientists respond, however, with "What about tomorrow's issues?" Many technical and legal experts are not convinced that today's disputes are the manifestations of transient legal problems. They are less confident in the ability of existing intellectual property law to be stretched to accommodate features of software that, they contend, are ill-served by the traditional models of legal protection. Vanderbilt University law professor Jerome H. Reichman went so far as to predict that continuing to stretch copyright and patent laws beyond their traditional scope will lead to "unsupportable restraints of trade and a breakdown of the world's intellectual property system."

Others troubled by the current state of affairs in the software industry called for a reassessment. "We need to think again and we need to be willing to question some of the most fundamental assumptions" of intellectual property law, said Randall Davis, associate director of the Artificial Intelligence Laboratory at the Massachusetts Institute of Technology.

Branscomb of Harvard suggested that the technical community's discomfort with the law may stem from a seeming incongruity between law and science. Therefore one might question the validity of applying legal precedents to what many technical experts believe is an unprecedented technology. "It is entirely possible," Branscomb said, "speaking from the scientist's point of view, that judges make correct and just findings in each case, while the opinions that give the rationale may look to the scientist as though they are stretching paradigms of early technologies to fit the frame of new ones, perhaps in an awkward way. Thus it is not unreasonable to ask, if the courts give us the right—that is, fair and just—answers, based on ill-fitting models: Does that matter?"

It does matter, according to Stanford University law professor Paul Goldstein, if the decisions do not clarify the law. "One of the law's roles in society is to reduce uncertainty," he said, distinguishing legal risks from the uncertainties of the marketplace, which are inherent to all forms of business. To software industry commentator Dyson, clarity and consistency may be as important as legal content. "I don't think anyone really cares what the rules are as long as it is clear what they are," she said. "The market can adjust."

So far, however, judicial decisions in software-related copyright infringement cases have not been consistent, maintained Ronald S. Laurie, head of the computer law group in Irell & Manella's Northern California office. This same problem, Laurie predicted, is likely to emerge in the application of patent law to software.

"I submit," he said, "that all of the issues that we are familiar with and that have caused such controversy and emotion in the copyright area concerning 'structure, sequence, and organization' and levels of abstraction are going to be reenacted in the patent context of the doctrine of equivalents." (See chapter 2 for a discussion of this doctrine.)

Patent protection, itself, exemplifies how the application of intellectual property law to software has changed. Following a 1972 Supreme Court decision, *Gottschalk, Acting Commissioner of Patents v. Benson et al.* (409 U.S. 63, 93 S. Ct. 253 [1972]), widely interpreted as rendering software as unpatentable subject matter separate from novel hardware, producers were discouraged from filing patent claims for their inventions. A 1981 Supreme Court decision, *Diamond v. Diehr* (450 U.S. 175), however, has been interpreted as restoring the protection for software that meets the stringent standards of patent law. Since then, the U.S. Patent and Trademark Office has been awarding patents for software-related inventions, and the number of claims filed for patents has been increasing steadily.

Many in the software industry welcome the protection, believing that patent law is the proper legal context in which to address some issues that, because of the presumed unavailability of patent protection, were forced into the domain of copyright law. Critics argue, however, that making patent protection available now amounts to changing the rules in the middle of the game. Some of these critics predict that patent protection will lead to a restructuring of the software industry.

"We don't have right now a clear notion about the boundaries of either patent or copyright [law]," said Pamela Samuelson, law professor at the University of Pittsburgh. "And we don't have a sense of the relationship between those two laws. . . . The lawyers out there have radically different views about that, and since they will give advice based on those very different views, we are in for some litigation in the future."

## UNPREDICTABLE FUTURE

Questions concerning intellectual property protection are a wedge that opens the door to an even larger and perhaps more complex set of issues that arise as society proceeds in the Information Revolution. "We still are in a stage of implementing the obvious in new ways," said Ernest E. Keet, partner at Vanguard Atlantic Ltd., the Connecticut-based merchant banking firm. "We really still have a long way to go to apply this new technology—the computer and software. . . ."

Today's debate focuses primarily on software as a tool for storing, processing, and presenting textual information in alphanumerical or graphical form. But tomorrow, the debate will almost certainly be expanded to include questions about rights of ownership to information itself and to the ideas embodied in that information. And that information will not only be blocks of text and tables of numbers, but also sounds and images combined and packaged in digital form. The possibilities for new products and service created by freeing information from the constraints of analog media—for example, sound from vinyl and tape, and images from photographs, tape, and film—are seemingly endless, barely hinted at by such terms as *multimedia*, *hypermedia*, *infotainment*, and *edutainment*.

"In the 30 years I have been in this business," said Harry Reinstein of Aion, "I know of no time that I could have accurately predicted where we would be in 5 years."

Reinstein is hardly alone. Consider a prediction made in the *Wall Street Journal* in a series of future-looking articles appearing during the mid-1960s: By the year 2000, the United States would have about 220,000 computers. Compare the reality: In 1990, an estimated 50 million computers were in U.S. homes and businesses. Wholly unanticipated by virtually everyone was the emergence of the personal computer, as well as a host of other information-related technologies. The more than 200-fold difference between projection and reality at the start of the decade leading into the next century is testimony, the *Wall Street Journal* said 25 years later, that the "electronic revolution has exploded beyond the dreams of even the most breathless early enthusiasts' visions of the future" (Miller, 1989).

To a great degree, prospects for realizing the possibilities now germinating in the minds of scientists, engineers, designers, and investors hinge on advances in software. If computers are truly to become the universal machine in the global information-based economy that is now evolving, it is software that will match the ever-increasing computational power of hardware with ever-more-sophisticated human needs and expectations.

For example, many experts believe that the next great leap in the problem-solving capabilities of computers will spring from parallel computing, in which interconnected machines, from two to tens of thousands, work on separate pieces of the same problem. Although embryonic versions of parallel computers already exist, the utility of such machines is constrained. "We do not have the algorithms that allow us to take some data-processing problem or transaction-processing problem and effectively break it up into small pieces and bring 1,000 or even 5,000 processors to bear on the problem," explained Michael O. Rabin, professor of computer science at Harvard University and Hebrew University. What is needed, he added, are "completely new algorithms." In Rabin's view, one potent incentive would be to provide stronger intellectual property protection. He expressed concern that without the incentive of exclusive rights of ownership, innovators might ignore the need for algorithms, and progress toward effective parallel computing and its numerous anticipated benefits might be impeded. Others do not share this view, citing the healthy growth of the research community in this area.

But a corollary to Rabin's assertion, one often raised as an objection to the patenting of algorithms and so-called software-related inventions, is that exclusive ownership of innovations grants monopoly power to inventors. Monopoly control, goes the argument, may cordon off the rest of the industry from building on fundamental breakthroughs. The public, in turn, might not reap the full commercial benefits of major advances until after the 17-year period of patent protection expires.

Other issues lurking on the horizon stem from the differing legal treatment given to different manifestations of information. Unlike numbers and words, noted Francis Fisher, images, under existing law, can be subject to rights. Yet, property rights in images may be inconsistent with the degree of freedom we want in communicating ideas that are incorporated in images.

Images are just the beginning. Observed Fisher, "We can even foresee the not distant day when the stuff of communications will include expressions and ideas that themselves are intelligent. That is, they will incorporate some sort of computer program. There may then be little distinction between what is a piece of software program and what is a piece of information on which that program operates."

In business and other realms of human activity where information is the fundamental item of value, notions of what software is will become all encompassing, predicted Esther Dyson. "The software business is virtually everybody," she said; "it is not a type of intellectual property. It is the representation of most intellectual property." Increasingly, software defines and embodies business practices, she said. For example, tax accounting and other procedures are represented and embodied not just in manuals but also in the applications that perform them.

## CONCLUSION

The path into the Information Age is not well marked, but innovation in software is necessary to pave the way and to ensure a steady rate of progress. Indeed, software not only sets the pace but also limits it. While the speed and power of computers double about every two years, software applications that harness this power for human uses evolve at a much slower rate, creating an ever-widening gap between expectation and reality.

"[C]ompared to computer hardware," said Harvard's Branscomb, "software is still the Achilles heel of the computer and communications industries, responsible for more shipment delays, cost overruns, and user frustrations—by a mile."

Branscomb later warned against the complacency that can arise when the software industry's past is used as the basis for projecting its future performance. "There is plenty of need," he said, "for new creative ideas, for the skills, tools, and effort to realize software ideas in code that is elegantly and reliably expressed. It is, in other words, not sufficient, in my opinion, to simply say that because software revenue doubles every five years and the United States has a preponderantly favorable position in world markets, then everything is therefore as good as it either could be or should be."

Intellectual property law figures prominently in the industry's future, setting the rules that guide the behavior of firms and individual inventors. Although optima are rarely achieved in real life, the law helps set the course toward achieving the goals that are deemed to be in the public interest. Among these goals, according to Branscomb, are encouraging the creation and diffusion of new concepts and ideas, as well as the dissemination of useful innovations based on these new ideas; encouraging the development of interoperability and connectivity in the interest of equitable public access to the fruits of information technology; generating the investments needed to advance the industry and the knowledge infrastructure on which the industry's technological progress is based; and assuring equitable allocation of the benefits of investment, creative genius, and hard work in an efficiently functioning marketplace.

"All of that needs to be accomplished on a worldwide level," Branscomb said, "because software is, of course, a major element in international trade, having not only the feature that it is cheap to replicate but also that it is cheap to communicate."

At this juncture, well-intentioned people disagree strongly on what legal environment is best for the technology, the industry, and, most important, for the public—today and tomorrow. What is clearly needed is balance: balance between private and public interest, balance between the need to protect the essence of innovation and the need to share for the sake of compatibility and interoperability, and balance between the need to foster leaps in the technology and the need to allow incremental improvements in the existing base of technology.

The legal uncertainties that cloud the software industry today indicate that the proper balance has yet to be achieved. Determining where to position the fulcrum of intellectual property law will not be easy. "I can see how too-protectionist a view could hurt our company," said Ingari of Lotus, "and, obviously, I can see how not enough protection could hurt our company."

Added ON Technology, Inc.'s Chairman Mitchell Kapor: "The digital revolution has just started. I cannot tell you how it is going to come out. I can see some of the dynamics. Market-mediated innovation is definitely the way to go, and my bottom line on the intellectual property front is let us not screw it up. The agonizing thing is, I cannot tell whether that means do nothing or do something radical. So, I am here to sort that out, but I know that the stakes are large."

## NOTES

1. Indeed, the Free Software Foundation (FSF) uses copyright in the form of a licensing agreement Stallman calls "Copyleft," but for an opposite purpose: to prevent its software from being incorporated into a priced product. FSF work revolves around products labeled GNU, for GNU's Not Unix. GNU software can run on Unix without being Unix and therefore without being subject to Unix licensing constraints (Garfinkel, 1991).

2. Use of multiple forms of protection may also stem from other causes. After all, a homeowner who installs strong locks and a burglar alarm does not do so because of uncertainty about the laws regarding burglary. However, the uncertainty that prevails in the software industry adds to the motivation for seeking multiple legal protections.

How do you get innovation to happen faster? Do you allow people really strong protection of their ideas so that it is worth the effort to take giant leaps? Or do you make protection weak so that innovation can be done all incrementally?
—Bruce Tognazzini, *Evangelist, Apple Computer, Inc.*

We have few phenomena more harmful to technological progress than [legal] uncertainty.
—Paul Goldstein, *Stella W. and Ira S. Lillick Professor of Law, Stanford University*

Copyright does not protect function. It does protect form, and if the two are bound together, we have a heck of a problem.
—Dennis S. Karjala, *Director, Center for the Study of Law, Science, and Technology, Arizona State University*

Until we have a clearer picture about the patent-copyright interface, I think we are going to be in some trouble. . . . Copyright is not supposed to pick up for what is to some extent the bad business of the patent system.
—Pamela Samuelson, *Professor of Law, University of Pittsburgh*

If we continue to stretch these paradigms [patent and copyright law] too far in order to accommodate the subject matters, . . . I'm afraid we are going to have a breakdown and a lot more problems than we think we are solving.
—Jerome H. Reichman, *Professor of Law, Vanderbilt University*

If you think you are getting inconsistent and irrational decisions in the courts now, create a new statute with no precedents and watch what happens.
—Ronald S. Laurie, *Partner, Irell & Manella*

# 2

# Background to Basic Legal Issues

Like other industries, the software industry operates within a large legal framework of which intellectual property laws are only a part, albeit a crucial one. Tax laws, the Uniform Commercial Code, and antitrust laws, among others, also regulate the behavior of software firms, and they too can influence the scope of inventive activity and the dissemination of innovations to the public.

Most legal debate in the software industry, however, is confined to copyright, patent, and trade secret laws. That the debate encompasses both the copyright and patent domains of intellectual property law seems to provide some support for the contention of software developers that their technology is unique. "Software is perhaps the first patentable subject matter which is also copyrightable," writes Duncan Davidson (Davidson, 1986, p. 1055). "No one yet knows what this means, if anything." But Vanderbilt University law professor Jerome Reichman questions the historical accuracy of this assertion. "Industrial designs," Reichman said, "are, to varying degrees, covered by both copyright and patent laws in all industrialized countries. Indeed, efforts to broaden copyright protection of industrial designs in the period 1900 to 1950 and the corresponding tensions this generated seem to anticipate the present tensions concerning software in almost every respect."

Under the three major domains of intellectual property law, protection is awarded to software not as a class, explained Ronald Laurie, head of Irell & Manella's computer law group, but on the basis of whether a program, language, interface, or other software element

21

"possesses attributes or characteristics that fall into one or more of the statutorily prescribed categories of protectable subject matter." For copyright law these hallmarks are expressions of ideas embodied in original works of authorship. Patent protection is awarded for products and processes that are novel, nonobvious, and useful. Trade secret law can be invoked to protect secret information that is used by a business and contributes to its commercial advantage. The extent to which software products satisfy these criteria is, of course, a matter of interpretation, which is where much of the uncertainty arises. Failure to satisfy the criteria means a work is available for all to use.

Within copyright law and, to some extent, patent law, these broad defining characteristics of protectable subject matter may have finer gradations. Particularly relevant to software are subcategories of copyrightable literary works, such as works of fiction, works of history, manuals, and telephone directories. The scope of protection varies according to the range of creative expression found in each type of work. (See Box 2.1.)

## COPYRIGHT

Copyright has been advanced as the preferred intellectual property protection for software in the United States and, with this nation's strong encouragement, internationally. In the 1980 amendments to the Copyright Act of 1976 (P.L. 94-553), Congress confirmed its intention that copyright protection applies to computer programs, but the 1976 revision of the federal copyright law did not stipulate the manner in which the protection applied. Through the 1980 Software Amendments, and acting on the recommendations of the National Commission on New Technological Uses of Copyrighted Works (CONTU), Congress placed software more squarely within the embrace of copyright by providing a definition of computer programs. In so doing, Congress continued a long tradition of extending copyright protection to new media of expression. Only books, maps, and charts were singled out in the first copyright law, passed in May 1790. Subsequent additions to the law included protection for musical compositions, photographs, drawings, statuary, paintings, motion pictures, and sound recordings. Reichman pointed out, however, that statutory authority to protect industrial designs—a category that, he believes, corresponds closely to software—was never implemented until 1954, and from 1958 to the present, the separability doctrine put forward by the U.S. Copyright Office "has effectively denied copyright protection to functional 'high-tech' designs of useful articles of high technology that have three-dimensional embodiments."

## BOX 2.1—LEGAL PROTECTIONS AS ISLANDS IN THE SEA OF FREE COMPETITION

To give forum participants the lay of the intellectual property law landscape, attorney Ronald S. Laurie of Irell & Manella used a metaphor-based model to describe the conceptual underpinnings of copyright and patent laws and their application.

Intellectual property protections are like islands in a sea of free competition. . . [I]f one is not able to place the fruits of one's investment, ingenuity, or creativity on one or more of the islands, then one is in the sea, and we all know what lives in the sea.

The model is, of course, simplistic and imperfect because it assumes that one can always tell when one is on dry land and one is in the water of unrestricted competition. In fact, the copyright island, which is low and sandy, has a gradual sloping beach called the merger of idea and expression. Thus, opinion may differ on how far out one has to wade before the boundary is crossed; that is, when the water is up to your neck, are you still on the island? This is especially true where the tide (read: inconsistent judicial decisions) varies with the time of day.

The patent island is a volcanic island with sheer cliffs rising to a commanding view of the surroundings. But the patent island also has a sandy beach, tucked away in a corner. It is called the doctrine-of-equivalents beach. I think we are going to hear a lot more about this area with the rising tide of software patents that are being issued and, of course, the consequent flood of software patent litigation.

One of the often-cited differences between patents and copyrights is that patents offer a much more predictable right—that patents have claims and, within certain limits, adverse parties can look at claims and decide whether they are on the right side or wrong side of the infringement rule. Whereas, as we all know, no one knows the scope of a copyright until a judge tells us what it is, and different judges will tell us different things about the same copyright.

I suggest that this reassuring element of predictability in the case of patent law is not as sure as you might think.

Indeed, Laurie predicted that interpretation of the doctrine of equivalents is likely to spawn controversies and appeal to levels of abstraction akin to those encountered in arguments of substantial similarity invoked in copyright infringement cases involving the structure, sequence, and organization of programs.

"I suggest," Laurie continued, "that as we discuss some of the difficult legal and technical issues, such as the protection of interfaces, communication protocols, and languages, the relevant question is not whether these areas are generally protectable as a class, but whether they may possess attributes or characteristics that fall into one or more of the statutorily prescribed categories of protectable subject matter."

Owners of copyrighted software are awarded exclusive rights to their works for varying periods, but typically with a 75-year maximum. Procedurally, copyright is an automatic protection, conferred as soon as an expression is fixed in a tangible medium, even if the work is never published. Registration with the Copyright Office is not required, nor is full disclosure necessary. To secure a registered copyright, the creator of a program need only submit descriptive materials on the first and last 25 written pages of the work, which usually do not constitute the entire program.

Copyright gives the creator control over several activities, including reproduction, distribution, and adaptation or translation into derivative works. Several recent and ongoing lawsuits[1] are testing the limits of these rights by raising the issue of what constitutes "substantial similarity," the basis for determining copyright infringement.

## Expressions, Ideas, and Functions

Copyright protection is extended only to expressions of ideas, not to the underlying ideas themselves. This distinction is especially critical for the software industry, where independent invention is common. Two designers may set out to tackle the same problem, each one creating different programs that accomplish essentially the same task. There are no grounds for copyright infringement if neither competitor copied the other's work. The situation is akin to one that might exist for two writers of romance novels, both of whom have the same general idea for a plot but whose finished works, although comparable at an abstract level, differ greatly in style, character development, and other literary aspects.

Allowance for independent invention distinguishes copyright law from patent law, which, as is described below, provides protection for ideas at some level. Thus copyright protection is said to be narrow, or "thin," because it permits duplication of function, a feature that becomes apparent when one shops for a word-processing program.

Not all copyrightable works are accorded the same extent of copyright protection. Artistic or fanciful works are considered to have a broad scope of protection by copyright because they are predominantly expressive in character. Factual works have a somewhat narrower scope of protection, because the facts and theories they contain are not protected by copyright. Works of a more functional character, such as architectural plans, recipe books, rule books, and the like, have traditionally been considered to contain little expression. Copyright law has regarded the functional content of such works to be among their unprotectable features, and hence the scope of protection for such works has been quite narrow, requiring exact or near-exact copying of the expressive aspects of the work for infringement to be found.

Some commentators on software copyright law would compare the complex structure of a computer program to the complex structure of novels, and would argue that just as the complex structure of a novel might be protectable expression under copyright law, so too should the complex structure of a program be protectable. Others would argue that the functional character of computer programs would suggest that a narrower scope of protection is appropriate under copyright law on the theory that the design of software is more akin to the engineering design for a bridge (which a copyright on a drawing would not protect) than to the design of a novel.

Software's peculiarities have spawned uneasiness in some quarters about the ability of copyright law to provide *effective protection*, a term with many interpretations. Indeed, Paul Goldstein, Stella W. and Ira S. Lillick Professor of Law at Stanford University, reflecting on the many changes in the industry, speculated that if CONTU had had the benefit of today's understanding of software, that body's recommendations would have been markedly different from those actually made a decade ago.

One source of vexation, at least for some, is the dissimilarity between software and its copyright analogue, literary works. Only rarely, for example, are computer programs sold or licensed in a written form even remotely understandable to people other than expert computer programmers. Most software is distributed as machine-readable object code, written as sequences of numbers. Except for the user interface, software—unlike literary works—does not reveal its expression to the consumer. Not all find this objection compelling. "The fact that it requires a certain competence to read a computer program with appreciation," Anthony L. Clapes, IBM's senior corporate counsel, has written, "merely puts computer programs in company with foreign language texts and other specialized literature: the ideas in them are not unintelligible; they simply do not yield themselves up to those untrained in the language in which the ideas are expressed" (Clapes, 1989, p. 143).

Also grounds for debate is the functionality of software, a property that further blurs copyright law's already fuzzy line between idea and expression. For practical purposes, idea and function are virtually synonymous, falling within the realm of patent law. Thus, in theory, copyright law does not protect the functionality of programs, but rather the expressions that result in the accomplishment of a given task. But the question of the extent to which copyright protects the functional elements software possesses, such as the command sequence for footnoting text, the arrangement of graphical symbols on a display, or other behavioral components of a program, will turn on the courts' judgments as to whether nonfunctional elements have been copied.

Goldstein attributed the legal uncertainty besetting the software industry to the "tension between the essential functionality of computer programs and copyright law's historic refusal to protect functional elements of otherwise qualifying works." Morton David Goldberg, of the New York law firm Schwab, Goldberg, Price, & Dannay, disagreed with this contention. He noted that copyright applies to several types of utilitarian works, including maps and charts. Pamela Samuelson of the University of Pittsburgh contended, however, that copyright law has traditionally not considered maps and charts to be "utilitarian" in character, for they merely convey information or display an appearance. "Works that have functions—in addition to conveying information or displaying an appearance—have been utilitarian in a copyright sense, and hence unprotectable by copyright," she said. "Computer programs are the first truly utilitarian work to be protectable by copyright."

Copyright law recognizes the "merger of expression and idea," an argument raised in many copyright-infringement cases but one that seems to have particular relevance for software. The merger doctrine holds that if an idea is inseparable from its expression, then only one or a few options exist for accomplishing a specific function. Therefore the expression is not protected, and copying is permissible. To do otherwise would grant monopoly control over an idea. Here, the machine side of software's dual nature becomes the focal point. The ability to do work, it is often argued, entangles idea and expression. If two programs are designed to perform the same function, will not the range of expression be limited, dictated by the task? After all, other machines—cars, for example—vary in style and detail, but their form is constrained by their function, necessitating many shared features.

The validity of the argument that expression is idea in software hinges on circumstances and, thus, judicial interpretation. In one case, for example, the court ruled that duplication of the sequence of data-input formats for a structural-analysis program did not constitute infringement, finding that the sequence was not expression, but an idea. The merger of idea and expression also was found to underlie the similarities in the "sequence and organization" of competing marketing information programs for cotton farmers. In this case, *Synercom Technology, Inc. v. Unni Computing Co.* (462 F. Supp. 1003 [N.D. Tex. 1978]), the need to conform with the conventions of the cotton market was thought to constrain the range of expression. The "merger" argument has also been rejected in many software cases, including those in which the issue was not literal copying but nonliteral similarity.

## What Constitutes Copyright Infringement?

Until only recently, intellectual property concerns in software were limited largely to literal copying. In the 1980s, new issues arose and, with them, a diversity of views on the scope of copyright protection. One boundary on this wide spectrum of opinion, the minimalist argument, posits that extending protection beyond the computer code and perhaps some audiovisual and tutorial features of the user interface will encourage monopoly and stifle competition. Maximalists, who reside at the opposite boundary, counter that such limited protection will remove the incentive to innovate.

Although some may align themselves with one view or the other, most software firms are not likely to endorse either one, preferring a practical view consistent with the realities and behavior of the industry. They recognize the need for programs to work with other programs, as demanded by users. Meeting this need will require using parts of others' software, as has been the industry's practice for much of its history. Overly broad protection would present a major obstacle, with each effort to create compatibility carrying the risk of a lawsuit. Underprotection, however, could create a paradise for free riders, producers of "knock-off," or cloned, programs.

Some lawyers see the law as steadily evolving to workable compromise that will accommodate software. In a review of decisions on the protectability of the "structure, sequence, and organization" of programs, Goldberg contends that the "developing body of case law in this area does provide helpful guidance, and will do so increasingly as more cases are decided" (Goldberg and Burleigh, 1989, p. 296). In her review of the situation, Samuelson draws the opposite conclusion, finding consensus extending only to copyrightability of computer programs. "Almost all of the important questions about what copyright protection means for software have yet to be answered definitively," she has written (Samuelson, 1988, p. 61).

Not surprisingly, these two legal experts also disagree on the appropriateness of, arguably, the most influential decision handed down thus far on the scope of copyright protection for software, that of the Third Circuit Court of Appeals in *Whelan Associates, Inc. v. Jaslow Dental Laboratory, Inc., et al.* (U.S. District Court for the Eastern District of Pennsylvania, 797 F. Supp. 1222 [1985]). Goldberg's and Samuelson's differences are explored below, with the aim of elucidating some of the disagreements in assessments of the applicability of copyright law to software.

At issue in *Whelan* was whether a business-management system developed for a dental laboratory and written for an IBM PC computer was a copy of a predecessor system that operated on an IBM Series 1 computer. The court held that "copyright protection of computer programs may extend beyond the programs' literal code to their structure, sequence, and organization." By the court's parsing of the dichotomy between idea and expression, an idea in a program is its "purpose or function"; the expression of the idea is "everything that is not necessary to that purpose or function." File and data structures, data flow, and the structure and sequence of screen displays that manifested program routines were construed as protectable expression.

In endorsing the appellate court's ruling that "substantial similarity" of nonliteral elements of programs can be proof of infringement, Goldberg suggests that limiting protection only to code "would be equivalent to permitting one freely to publish a copyrighted English-language novel in an unauthorized French translation, or to dramatize it or make it into a motion picture without authorization" (Goldberg and Burleigh, 1989, p. 301). He also dismisses arguments that the *Whelan* decision confers protection on all elements of a program except its underlying idea. Goldberg notes that the court based its finding of comprehensive nonliteral similarity on its review of data structures, screen outputs, and five subroutines or modules. The court considered the possibility of "merger of idea and expression" but dismissed it, pointing to evidence cited by the district court that competing, commercially available programs had different structures and designs and yet had the same purpose. As evidence that the *Whelan* decision does not imply blanket protection to programs, Goldberg points out that a number of plaintiffs have lost "structure, sequence, and organization" cases decided after *Whelan*.

Goldberg also concurs with the court's rejection of the view that the incremental nature of progress in software development necessitates some copying. The court did not see any qualitative difference between progress in the development of software and progress in other areas of science and the arts where copyright law applies.

Samuelson, in contrast, contends that the *Whelan* decision not only takes the "radical step" of regarding the overall structure of a program, which she regards as a functional design, to be protectable expression under copyright law, but more radically than that, adopts a test for software copyright infringement that would recognize everything about a program except its general function or purpose as copyrightable "expression." Samuelson points out that the appellate court quoted with approval a passage from the trial court decision that described as protectable expression "the manner in which the program operates, controls, and regulates the computer in receiving, assembling, calculating, retaining, correlating, and producing useful information." Such wording, she adds, would make the functionality of a program into protectable expression, ignoring copyright law's exclusion from protection of processes, procedures, methods of operation, and systems that might be described in a copyrighted work. Functional processes and designs have traditionally been within the domain of patent law, not copyright.

Finally, Samuelson suggests that applying the *Whelan* decision's test for differentiating between idea and expression seems to have "swept" algorithms "into the fold of 'expression.'" Within recent years, the U.S. Patent and Trademark Office has begun awarding patents for "method algorithms" embodied in software-related inventions, providing protection for 17 years. However, if the *Whelan* decision is to be taken seriously, copyright protection and its 75 years of coverage could be extended to algorithms, Samuelson maintains, "particularly if a software copyright plaintiff's lawyer is astute enough not to call the algorithm an algorithm, but rather the structural backbone of the software."

To Samuelson, copyright law's aversion to technology is manifested in the way the courts have chosen to address software-related issues. Virtually all courts have treated software entirely by analogy to literary works, ignoring its status as technology. While acknowledging that certain aspects of software fall clearly within the province of copyright law, Samuelson advises that, for the law to embrace the technological aspects of software, fundamental changes in the copyright system would be required. "Judges have been blind to the fact that software is a technology and that progress in the field of technological arts may more easily be impeded by strong copyright protection than might be the case in the field of the literary arts," she maintains.

## TRADE SECRET

A commonly used protection, trade secrets are often used in conjunction with copyright, which serves as a first line of defense in the event that a program is "reverse engineered" by a competitor. Indeed, the Copyright Office accommodates the software industry's heavy reliance on trade secrets by allowing registration with descriptive, identifying materials that do not reveal confidential information.

Under state trade secret laws, firms use licensing contracts that stipulate conditions under which software can be used, copied, modified, translated, or transferred. Such contractual prohibitions can be circumvented, however, and enforcement problems are magnified by the growing prevalence of distributed computing, which makes licensed programs easily accessible to nonlicensed users. The reverse-engineering proscriptions are not necessarily binding on nonlicensed users, a problem with potentially disastrous consequences for innovators who rely on this form of protection alone. Unlike machines and other technologies that have a material manifestation, software, as already noted, can be disassembled and reassembled into a form that bears little resemblance to the copied work, thus defeating the trade secret protection. In addition, a competitor could independently develop and then patent a software-related process that a company had protected through trade secret. Since patent law does not recognize trade secrets as prior art, the original innovator would be forced either to stop selling the software product or to license the process from the competitor that holds the patent.

Sellers of off-the-shelf software often attempt to impose agreements—"shrink-wrap licenses"—upon purchasers opening the plastic wrapper that encases the disk on which the program is stored.[2] Buyers are allowed to make archival copies, but self-executing shrink-wrap licensing agreements may prevent them from copying the program and distributing it to others. To treat programs sold in volumes of hundreds of thousands and even millions as trade secrets, according to one commentator, "offends common sense—the fact that so much copying takes place indicates how few users take the agreement seriously" (Branscomb, 1988, p. 43).

Software firms are becoming increasingly concerned about the viability of contracts applied to large numbers of users. On the one hand, wide-scale distribution may render the claim of trade secret meaningless. On the other, there are fears that the "first sale doctrine" will undermine licensing agreements. Under the doctrine, the purchaser of a copyrighted work is free to disseminate that work, although copying is limited to certain prescribed circumstances. Such circumstances include those cited in the copyright law's "fair use doctrine," which allows copying for the purposes of research and criticism. Both doctrines, some observers speculate, could serve as the means to erode the scope of trade-secret protection, as well as copyright protection. Another concern is that federal copyright law will preempt state trade secret laws. Indeed, in a closely related area, a federal appellate court in Louisiana ruled in 1988 that portions of that state's shrink-wrap enforcement law are preempted by copyright law (Samuelson, 1988).

Uncertainty over the legitimacy of shrink-wrap licenses hangs over the entire industry, said Charles M. Geschke, president and chief operating officer of Adobe Systems, Inc. He warned of the potential danger that competitors could "take what I have licensed to them and use it as a weapon to come back and compete with me by [automated] reverse engineering. That is very hard, from a developer's point of view, to accept as a really fair form of competition."

## PATENT

In the 1972 case *Gottschalk v. Benson*, the U.S. Supreme Court ruled that mathematical algorithms were not patentable, spawning the view that software-related inventions, the essence of which is often an algorithm, were not eligible for patent protection. In fact, CONTU, in its analysis of potential intellectual property protections for software, shared this perception and dismissed patents as an option (Samuelson, 1988). A year after Congress enacted CONTU's copyright recommendations, however, the Supreme Court opened the patent door to software, ruling in *Diamond, Commissioner of Patents and Trademarks v. Diehr et al.* (Supreme Court of the United States, 450 U.S. 175 [1981]) that the use of an algorithm does not render unpatentable an invention that would otherwise be eligible for the protection (Kahin, 1989).

The decision in *Diamond v. Diehr*, which concerned the patentability of a rubber-curing process directed with the aid of a computer program, was hardly an unequivocal endorsement of the patenting of software. Some commentators suggest that the wording in the 5 to 4 decision allows the court sufficient room to reassess the issue in the future. But in the nearly 10 years since *Diamond v. Diehr*, the high court has chosen not to revisit the matter. Meanwhile, the number of software-related patents awarded by the Patent and Trademark Office rose from none in 1980 to about 200 annually in recent years, according to estimates prepared for the Computer Law Committee of the State Bar of Texas (cited in Brian Kahin, "The Case Against Software Patents," unpublished paper, 1989, p. 1).

As is true for the copyrightability of software, the patentability of software-related inventions may be viewed as a boon or a bane, depending on one's perspective. A simplified pro-patent argument holds that the protection is most appropriate for addressing the technological aspects of software, while providing a powerful incentive for innovation. The contrary argument views patents as anticompetitive because, unlike copyrights, they do not allow for independent invention, and as increasing the risk of litigation because of the secrecy of the patent-approval process.

## Characteristics of Patents

A patent provides 17 years of protection to owners of inventions—works that are nonobvious, novel, and useful—in exchange for full disclosure of the inventions at the time of application. Because it precludes independent invention, patent law is said to provide "thicker" protection than does copyright law, forcing competitors to "invent their way around" a patented innovation.

Donald S. Chisum, professor of law at the University of Washington, maintained that, compared to copyrights, patents are a "nobler" form of protection. By "dangling out a reward, the right to exclude others from using useful processes and products," he said, the first-to-file requirement and its winner-take-all result hasten the pace of innovation. Even companies with large market shares cannot be content to rest on past accomplishments because, according to Chisum, they run the risk of being "completely knocked out of the market by a technological innovation that is developed and patented" by a competitor. Moreover, the disclosure requirement provides competitors with a clear understanding of the inventive hurdle they must leap to compete with the patent holder, thereby setting the stage for the next round of innovation.

Unlike the protection provided by copyright law, patent protection extends to functionality. Different implementations of an idea or incremental improvements to a patented invention are not eligible for protection because they do not satisfy the patent law's requirement for nonobviousness. Indeed, such implementations or improvements, if undertaken by a competitor, constitute infringement of the patented innovation. In theory, the monopoly grant awarded to the patent holder fosters more efficient development within industry by discouraging duplication of effort.

The scope of patent protection is subject to uncertainty, however, in the guise of the doctrine of equivalents, patent law's counterpart to copyright's doctrine of substantial similarity. Determining whether two inventions are substantially similar is a matter for judicial interpretation, and the reasoning applied in the few software-related cases that have reached the courts thus far has not always been consistent.

"Courts are essentially schizophrenic about patents," Chisum explained. "On the one hand, we say that it is the function of the patent claim to delineate what is covered. If you don't claim it, you don't have any exclusive rights over it, and yet on the other hand, they [the courts] apply . . . the doctrine of equivalents. In some circumstances, something that literally does not conform to the verbal statement in the patent is nevertheless found to be an infringement, and as you can imagine, that is a great source of ambiguity."

Added Ronald Laurie, of Irell & Manella, "I think we are going to be hearing a lot more about this area [doctrine of equivalents] with the rising tide of software patents that are being issued and, of course, the consequent flood of software-patent litigation."

Proponents of patent protection for software suggest that some of the issues now being contested in copyright cases stem from the presumed unavailability of the protection following the Supreme Court decision in *Gottschalk v. Benson*. People have tried to "stretch the boundaries of copyright protection to fill in for the fact that no one [had] patent protection," said John Shoch, general partner at the Asset Management Co. He cited the current spate of "look and feel" cases as symptomatic of the problems that arise when copyright law is used to address issues that belong in the domain of patent law.

"[W]e find ourselves in this tremendous fight about look and feel, and function, and interfaces in the copyright domain, which is absolutely the wrong place to have much of this fight," Shoch contended. The proper legal arena for these issue, he added, is patent law. In his view, the software industry will benefit if patent protection is made fully available, alongside copyright and trade secret protection.

Not everybody sees the emergence—or reemergence—of patent protection as a positive development. Brian Kahin, adjunct research fellow at Harvard University, argued that the late arrival of patent protection is potentially disruptive, suggesting that the virtual absence of patenting until recent years may undermine the highly decentralized structure of the software industry.

"If software had clearly been protectable from the outset, there would be no surprise, no defeated expectations," Kahin has written (Brian Kahin, "The Case Against Software Patents," unpublished paper, 1989, pp. 8-9). "But now it appears that the industry may have to be reshaped to fit the patent system and that the rapid development of software products may have to be slowed to fit the review, processing, and publication cycle of the Patent and Trademark Office."

Yet, the nature of software is such that many of its components satisfy patent law's eligibility criteria, Laurie maintained, noting the interchangeability of function between software and hardware. "If you say that hardware is patentable and software isn't," he said, "then you are saying to developers and to engineers that depending . . . on how they resolve the design trade-off, they may get protection or they won't get protection" even though they are solving identical problems in virtually identical ways. "That is injecting, in my opinion, too many legal considerations." Adds IBM vice president for systems and programming Peter Schneider, "The most disturbing part about patent protection as it relates to software is that it is an indicator of how fast the legal community changes its mind."

## What Is Patentable?

What is eligible for patent protection? According to the U.S. Supreme Court decision in *Diamond, Commissioner of Patents and Trademarks v. Chakrabarty* (447 U.S. 303, 100 S. Ct. 2204 [1980]), Congress intended patent law to embrace "anything under the sun that is made by man"—anything, that is, falling into any one of the four categories of statutory subject matter: process, machine, manufacture, or composition of matter. Among the items not sheltered by the broad umbrella of patentable subject matter are laws of nature, physical phenomena, abstract ideas, "mental steps," and methods of doing business.

Software clearly qualifies as a human-made artifact. But the technology's critical dependency on mathematical algorithms, which patent law views as akin to laws of nature, positions software right at the drip line of the umbrella of patentable subject matter. Thus the Supreme Court ruling in *Gottschalk v. Benson*, holding that "an algorithm, or mathematical formula, is like a law of nature, which cannot be the subject of a patent," was widely interpreted as excluding software from patent protection. In *Diamond v. Diehr*, the high court did not reverse its 1972 decision, but rather it said the mere presence of an algorithm did not automatically render a process or machine ineligible for a patent. It did not say categorically, however, that computer programs are patentable. Nevertheless, the highest specialized court in the domain of patent law, the Court of Customs and Patent Appeals (CCPA; the predecessor to the Court of Appeals for the Federal Circuit), "has held that computer processes are statutory unless they fall within a judicially determined exception" (U.S. Patent and Trademark Office, 1989, p. 6).

Using the somewhat equivocal guidance provided by the courts, the Patent and Trademark Office has developed an operational concept of what software elements are eligible for patents, giving rise to such terms as *software-related inventions, computer processes,* and *computer algorithms*—a classification distinct from unpatentable mathematical algorithms. The upshot, according to Michael S. Keplinger, an attorney advisor in the Office of Legislation and International Affairs at the Patent and Trademark Office, is that patents are not awarded for computer software. "We grant patents," he explained, "on computer processes, processes that may be implemented in a computer, just as they might be implemented in a production-line machine or in any other hardware embodiment." Abstract descriptions of computer processes do not qualify, Keplinger added. Only specific implementations of processes in hardware are eligible.

Nor does the Patent and Trademark Office's parsing render mathematical algorithms patentable. "We used to say that we didn't issue patents on algorithms," Keplinger explained, "but you can't say that, because any process is an algorithm. It is a difficult line to [draw]— for a patent examiner to determine where you draw the dividing line between a purely mathematical algorithm, which we won't issue a patent for, and a process that may be expressed in mathematical terms," which will receive a patent if it is sufficiently useful, novel, and nonobvious.

To help inventors and their attorneys, the Patent and Trademark Office recently published a legal analysis that describes a two-part test to determine whether a product or process containing an algorithm is eligible for patent protection. The test is the evolutionary product of decisions made by the Supreme Court and the CCPA (U.S. Patent and Trademark Office, 1989).

## Test for Patentability

The first step, determining the presence of a "mathematical algorithm," is relatively straightforward, although, on occasion, ascertaining whether an algorithm is included in a claim may require some interpretation. The description of a mathematical algorithm, defined as a procedure for solving a given type of mathematical problem, is inconsequential. It may be in the form of a mathematical equation or it may be described in prose. More significant is the nature of the claim, whether it is for a process or a machine. By themselves, algorithms are considered processes that are ineligible for patents. To enhance their chances for securing a patent, some innovators have filed machine, or apparatus, claims that typically describe an algorithm as a means for accomplishing a task. The label is often not convincing. The applicant must demonstrate that functions described in the claim can be performed with a specific apparatus only. Most applicants fail to prove this specificity, and so most machine claims embodying algorithms are treated as process claims.

The second step in the test, distinguishing "between patentable process and unpatentable principle," is not free of ambiguity, as the Supreme Court noted in the 1978 case *Parker v. Flook* (437 U.S. 584, 593; 198 U.S.P.Q. 193, 198-99 [1978]). Lacking definitive tests for making the distinction, the Patent and Trademark Office's analysis offers several guidelines that it "synthesized" from court decisions. Apparently key to the final determination, however, is the specificity with which an algorithm is applied to steps in a physical process or, in the case of a machine claim, to physical elements. This implied penchant for specificity stems from the desire to prevent preempting the use of an algorithm in other applications. That is precisely the result the Supreme Court sought to avoid in *Gottschalk v. Benson* and in *Parker v. Flook*, noting in the former case that "the practical effect" of excluding broad areas of use "would be a patent on the algorithm itself."

Especially influential here is a CCPA decision in an appeal of a claim denied by the Patent and Trademark Office, *Lever Brothers Company v. Thrift-D-Lux Cleaners, Inc.* (U.S. Court of Customs and Patent Appeals, 46 CCPA 798, 263 F.2d 842 [1959]). In *In re* Abele (684 F.2d 902, 214 U.S.P.Q. (BNA) 682 [CCPA 1982]), the CCPA suggested reviewing a claim without the algorithm. If the remaining process or machine qualifies as patentable subject matter, according to the court, then inclusion of an algorithm should not alter that determination. This procedure does not suggest, the Patent and Trademark Office stresses, that the inventive merits of the claim be assessed in this manner, since the entire process or machine must be evaluated to determine novelty and nonobviousness.

A computer process is not patentable if the claim merely lists potential applications. The Patent and Trademark Office, referring to the decision in *Parker v. Flook*, classifies such a listing as "insignificant or non-essential post-solution activity." Similarly, a process is not eligible if the end product is simply the recording of the results of a calculation, nor is a process that is confined to assembling data for assigning values to variables in an algorithm. If, however, data gathering is dictated by steps other than the algorithm, then the process may be eligible. Less ambiguous are processes that transform "something physical into a different form," as compared with those that, by means of computation, transform one set of numbers into a different set. Thus the court has ruled as patentable a process that transforms "spherical seismic signals" into a "form representing the earth's response to cylindrical or plane waves" (*Mehmet Turhan Taner, Fulton Koehler, Nigel A. Anstey and Michael J. Castelberg*, U.S. Court of Customs and Patent Appeals, 681 F.2d 787 [1982]). Such processes have been deemed analogous to the conversion of sound into electrical signals or other transformations of signals accomplished with electrical circuitry.

Once one leaves the fairly well defined domain of signal transformation and other discretely defined processes, uncertainty begins to intrude. For example, the Patent and Trademark Office notes that claims can be rejected as nonstatutory if the process represents business methods and mental steps, and "not a true computer process." Amplifying this point, the analysis cites a 1977 appeal (*Gaetan de Coye de Castelet*, U.S. Court of Customs and Patent Appeals, 562 F.2d 1236 [1977]): "Claims to nonstatutory processes do not automatically and invariably become patentable upon incorporation of reference to apparatus." But closer examination may determine such machine-implemented processes to be eligible. Indeed, the analysis goes on to say that several cases decided during the 1970s indicate that "machine or computer implementation of mental steps is statutory subject matter." Thus the CCPA deemed a computer process translating natural languages as patentable. Indeed, a substantial number of people in the software industry would probably concur with that opinion.

Grounds for greater debate may be a federal district court's decision regarding the patentability of a cash management system. If carried out manually, the system would not be eligible, but in its incarnation as a computer process, the system was found to qualify for protection. The court concluded that the process was not a business method but rather a "method of operation on a computer to effectuate a business activity" (*Paine, Webber v. Merrill Lynch*, 564 F. Supp. 1369, 218 U.S.P.Q. 220 [1983]). This distinction has mystified some in the industry.

### Coherent or Incoherent?

Meanwhile, despite the great effort expended by the courts and the Patent and Trademark Office to elucidate the nature of computer processes, some legal experts believe that the system can be manipulated to secure patent protection for mathematical algorithms. "As long as you don't call it an algorithm," said Chisum, "it is probably going to be patentable as a method, even though it really is an algorithm." The Supreme Court decision in *Gottschalk v. Benson*, he maintained, remains as a source of lingering confusion and incoherence, making such behavior necessary. To avoid invoking that decision, Chisum explained, patent attorneys "dress up" algorithms "with language that makes it into a method or process."

Mitchell D. Kapor of ON Technology, Inc., questioned the "intellectual coherence" of the patent system as characterized by Chisum. "[O]ne's business strategy may hinge on legal subtleties that are apparently disconnected from anything that makes sense to us," he said.

Another technical expert who fails to see conceptual clarity in the law's and the Patent and Trademark Office's treatment of algorithms is Allen Newell, a professor of computer science at Carnegie Mellon University. In an oft-cited article, Newell maintains, "The models we have for understanding the entire arena of the patentability of algorithms are inadequate—not just somewhat inadequate, but fundamentally so. They are broken" (Newell, 1986). Many of Newell's numerous criticisms center on the practical utility of most discoveries of computer science, an attribute that distinguishes the field from other research areas. "With rare exceptions," he writes, "scientific knowledge in computer science is in the form of means-end relationships—what to do to obtain something of value. Indeed this is just the essence of algorithms: what to do to perform a task. But algorithms, far from being an applied part of computer science, are at the center of its basic theoretical structure."

Therein lies a problem. It is plausible, Newell maintains, that for any process a limited number of reasonably efficient algorithms may exist. To grant monopoly over these efficient processes would impose a "stranglehold" on additive inventive activity that would otherwise build on important algorithms. In some technological domains, Newell speculates, all inventive activity may involve algorithms, and the entire realm of invention "would come to reside in a computer."

"If methods and processes over large technological domains become an exercise in algorithms," Newell explains, "then it is extraordinarily dangerous not to patent algorithms." Therefore, patents for algorithms may indeed be necessary, but that determination cannot be made with existing legal models of algorithms, he argues.

At the forum, Michael O. Rabin, a professor of mathematics and computer science at Harvard University and Hebrew University, strongly endorsed patent protection for mathematical algorithms because of their increasingly influential role in technology development. Algorithms, he said, are human inventions, not discoveries, which are unpatentable. Incentives and, therefore, protection are required to encourage people to aspire to tackle important problems whose solutions require new algorithms.

If algorithms are viewed from this perspective, Rabin said, patent criteria that necessitate linking an algorithm to a specific process or a specific device will be found to be too confining. "I have a feeling," he said, "that this is going to be too narrow," reflecting, perhaps, the time lag between technological advance and legal response. "We do understand devices, linkages, values, and differentials, and so on, but we are moving to the edge of information and to the edge where the tools . . . are mathematical," he continued. "Yes . . ., they are ephemeral, but they are all powerful, and I think these innovations . . ., these tools, deserve at least as much protection as . . . the protection afforded to the cap on a soft-drink bottle, and so, this is my proposition and my plea."

## THE INTERNATIONAL SITUATION

With the strong urging of the United States, many foreign nations—more than 40 as of late 1989—have adopted copyright or roughly equivalent protection for software. Although a smaller number of countries, including Japan, also allow patenting of software, there is growing international consensus that copyright should be the primary means of protection and that software should be treated like other copyrighted works, according to Keplinger, of the U.S. Patent and Trademark Office.

Two treaties, the Paris Convention for the Protection of Industrial Property and the Berne Convention for the Protection of Literary and Artistic Property, serve as the basis for international treatment of copyrighted and patented works and are administered primarily by the UN's World Intellectual Property Organization (WIPO). Most relevant to software is the Berne Convention, which the United States signed in 1988, thereby supplanting most, but not all, of the bilateral copyright agreements it had negotiated with other nations. Signatories to the Berne Convention agree to meet a minimum set of legal requirements and, more important, to afford "national treatment" to works produced by authors in member nations. Thus French authors of computer programs imported into the United States, for example, are awarded the same exclusive rights of ownership as U.S. software publishers who market their programs domestically. Conversely, U.S. software exported to France would be accorded full copyright protection under that nation's laws.

Keplinger noted that the international conventions do not explicitly mention software. Rather, protection for the technology stems from treaty wording that applies comprehensively to works of authorship. Although a WIPO initiative to develop a model law specific to the protection of software has not advanced, Keplinger said, one can "make a credible argument that the Berne Convention already requires its members to protect computer programs under copyright law, because they are generally regarded as protectable subject matter by countries that have addressed the problem." (See Box 2.2.)

Nevertheless, copyright laws do vary among nations, creating some uncertainty. Keplinger explained that a German Supreme Court ruling seems to require "a relatively high degree of originality for computer programs, with the result that some German lawyers feel that many programs will be ineligible for protection under this high standard. . . ." France has chosen to classify software as an applied art—rather than a literary art—and provides protection for a term of 25 years, compared with 50 years for most other treaty nations. However, the European Economic Community (EEC), of which France is a member, is preparing a directive on intellectual property protection for software that may (based on the content of drafts) propose full copyright coverage for software, including protection for 50 years.

---

**BOX 2.2—UNFAIR COMPETITION LAW**

In many countries, slavish imitation of intangible creations is still regarded—overtly or covertly—as a wrongful act in its own right, according to Jerome H. Reichman of Vanderbilt University. This controversial business tort, known as misappropriation, is widely recognized in state unfair competition laws, but these laws often conflict with federal intellectual property protections. As a result, the U.S. Supreme Court has on several occasions reduced the scope of state laws. Recently, Switzerland enacted a new misappropriation law deliberately aimed at preventing theft of new technology. This use of unfair competition law in this capacity has greatly influenced foreign intellectual property law, Reichman said, but so far, it has attracted little attention in the United States.

Reichman suggested that it might be easier and more effective to add an antipiracy clause to the Paris Convention (to which more than 90 countries adhere) than to "stuff" computer programs into the Berne Convention, which governs literary and artistic works. (See text.) This would be feasible, he said, if a GATT agreement on intellectual property ultimately strengthened international arrangements covered by the Paris Convention, which covers industrial property.

---

The proposed EEC directive, which specifies how copyright protection applies to software, contains a controversial measure that, opponents contend, would "drastically limit rivals' ability to decipher software interfaces and build compatible products" (Verity, 1990, pp. 138 and 140). Proponents argue that the measure would be an effective deterrent to "commercial copying" of software.

In December 1990, the Council of Ministers of the European Community adopted a "Common Position" on the Directive on the Legal Protection of Computer Programs, which permits more extensive reverse analysis than earlier drafts of the directive. The Common Position would permit decompilation to the extent necessary to develop competitive—but themselves noninfringing—interoperable products. A final directive is expected to be adopted by late summer or early fall, 1991, after it is reviewed again by the European Parliament, the Council of Ministers, and possibly the Commission of the European Community.

Meanwhile, Japan has excluded algorithms, rules, and programming languages from copyright protection, a revision that observers inside and outside of Japan speculate will abet widespread copying. A 1989 decision by the Japanese high court, the first ruling under the amended copyright law, found that copying a program's "processing flow"—the court's interpretation of an algorithm—did not constitute infringement, according to Dennis S. Karjala, director of Arizona State University's Center for the Study of Law, Science, and Technology. Compared with the ruling in the U.S. case of *Whelan v. Jaslow*, however, the Japanese court's decision "did not go nearly as far in protecting nonliteral features of programs," Karjala said.

To assure reasonable levels of protection for software and other forms of intellectual property worldwide, the United States and other nations have proposed including an intellectual property code in the General Agreement on Tariffs and Trade (GATT), which has about 100 nations as signatories. Incorporated into this proposal are clarifications of the rights accorded to owners of software under copyright law, as well as mechanisms for enforcement, which are lacking in the Berne Convention. A benefit of addressing intellectual property issues through the GATT, Keplinger said, is the treaty's dispute-resolution process, which entails convening a panel to determine whether a member state is living up to its obligations. In contrast, disputes that arise under the Paris and Berne Conventions are referred to the World Court, which does not have enforcement powers. While Keplinger said that inconsistencies and other deficiencies in international conventions for protecting intellectual property need to be improved, he strongly advised against measures that would deviate from international norms of copyright and patent protection. Abandoning these norms, rather than "fine-tuning" them, he warned, would jeopardize past progress in "getting meaningful levels of protection for our works and our technology abroad."

## NOTES

1. *Lotus Development Corporation v. Paperback Software International and Stephenson Software, Limited* (Civil Action No. 87-76-K, U.S. District Court for the District of Massachusetts, 740 F. Supp. 37 [June 28, 1990]), for example, addressed this issue in considerable detail. In October 1990, Paperback agreed not to appeal the decision (Keefe, 1991).

2. The legal status of shrink-wrap licenses is quite uncertain. One school of legal analysts believes they are clearly unenforceable without the consent of the buyer. Others believe this is still an open question.

What is it that we want to protect? First . . . is the brilliant invention, the idea, the notion that makes a new product and the insight that makes a whole new industry. . . . [T]he second thing we want to protect is the investment and the hard work. This is the grunt work. This is the pick-and-shovel engineering that turns the idea, the prototype, into a reliable, distributable, maintainable, documented, supportable product.

—Robert Spinrad, *Director, Corporate Technology, Xerox Corp.*

Since the Industrial Revolution we have had copyright to protect printed works and patent to protect machines made out of iron and steel. The problem is that software is really some of both. It is the first technology that has content.

—Mitchell D. Kapor, *Chairman, ON Technology, Inc.*

We have managed to lay down the flooring, so we don't have to stand in the mud. But the problem is we are trying to build cathedrals and the ceiling is still a ways up there. . . . Every time the floor comes up a little bit, the ceiling shoots up higher because aspirations keep getting higher.

—Randall Davis, *Associate Director, Artificial Intelligence Laboratory, Massachusetts Institute of Technology*

We have some wonderful arrogance in thinking that the world of software is so much different from mechanical engineering or the new biological and pharmaceutical disciplines. I, in fact, don't believe that is the case.

—John F. Shoch, *General Partner, Asset Management Co.*

# 3

# Is Software a Special Case?

For the purposes of the law, the relevant question is not whether software is different from other technologies and creative works that now come under the protective umbrella—it clearly is. Rather, the issue is whether software is so different that extensions or modifications of existing legal constructs are needed. Opinions abound on this question. Said Stanford University law professor Paul Goldstein, "Any time you are dealing with creative artists—and that, to an extent, is what you are talking about here—you are talking about people who genetically believe their work is different. . . . [T]he history of copyright suggests that those differences will be taken account of." Some experts in patent law echoed that reasoning.

Not all legal and technical experts attending the forum, however, were as confident in the providence of the legal system. For example, Mitchell Kapor, chairman of ON Technology, suggested that software is so "fundamentally different" from works on paper, the traditional realm of copyright law, that a "first-principle reconsideration" of the law may be more appropriate than determining "how to stretch copyright." Added Pamela Samuelson, law professor at the University of Pittsburgh, confusion about the expressive and functional elements of software contributes to the blurring of boundaries between copyright law and patent law.

## THE PROCESS

Depending on whom you ask, software is either *written, engineered, built,* or *grown*—each term capturing some aspect of the process. Per-

43

haps the most distinguishing feature of the process, however, is the insignificance of manufacturing as a component, a factor that underlies software's inherent vulnerability to copying.

"It is all design and no manufacture," explained Randall Davis, associate director of the Massachusetts Institute of Technology's Artificial Intelligence Laboratory. "Reproducing it is trivial. Building it . . . is the hard part. There is no significant added effort in building [a multitude of identical products] once you have built the first one."

The process is so different from that in other fields of engineering, Duncan M. Davidson has written, that it warrants revising Thomas Edison's famous characterization of invention as "one percent inspiration and ninety-nine percent perspiration." For software, according to Davidson, the proper equation may be "fifty percent inspiration and fifty percent perspiration" (Davidson, 1986, p. 1062).

While those in the field may quibble about the exact proportions of the creativity and toil that go into a successful software product, they do agree that both elements are essential. A "brilliant idea" gives birth to a new product and, perhaps, even an entire industry, Xerox's Robert Spinrad explained, but its potential cannot be realized without the "pick-and-shovel engineering that turns the idea, the prototype, into a reliable, distributable, maintainable, documented, supportable product."

To Kapor, design is an underappreciated element of software development, even though it is the primary determinant of a product's value. "I believe more and more of the economic fortunes of computer companies . . . [will] depend on how well designed the programs are, not merely on how well they are implemented," he said. "[W]e had better worry seriously, if that is the crucial economic element, about what we want to do about protecting the design of software, independent of all the other factors."

Jerome Reichman agreed with Kapor and predicted that no long-term solution to the legal problems associated with protecting software will emerge until lessons drawn from the 200-year history of design protection law are brought to bear on this new subject matter, which he calls "industrial literature."

Yet, the importance of those other factors should not be diminished. An idea, no matter how brilliant, will not reach commercial fruition, Spinrad said, without the "detailed work" that goes into making a practical marketable product. Design and implementation, however, are not separate spheres of software development. The two activities are interactive.

The path that leads from idea to product is usually circuitous, and progress can be painstakingly slow, as evidenced by the field's apparent resistance to major enhancements in productivity. In fact, software development entails going down many paths simultaneously, retracing one's steps, and starting out anew with a slightly revised objective in mind. Dan Bricklin, co-developer of VisiCalc, the first spreadsheet program for a personal computer, broke the process down into eight stages, as described in Box 3.1. "This is a constant iterative process," he said, and testing is nearly continuous. "Every time you test, you end up changing your design, your constraints [such as the amount of memory required or the speed of executing an operation], or your statement of the problem." Each cycle results, Bricklin explained, in "greater understanding of what you are trying to do."

"You can't just specify [a product], give it to a coder, and say it will work," he added. "You will end up with lousy programs."

The seeming circularity of software development stems from a difficulty that exists from the outset—the difficulty of clearly defining the problem that the product is intended to solve. Studies of the process suggest that at least 50 percent of the errors that arise during development stem not from coding mistakes, according to MIT's Davis, but rather from inadequate formulation of the problem and incomplete understanding of human behavior.

"We try to build things," he said, "and we really don't know what they are until we start to build them. So, one punch line here is, it isn't the programming that is hard; it is figuring out what we're trying to do that is hard." Consequently, the problem that motivated the development effort may not be fully specified until the final code is written. And even then, future changes are inevitable because customers are bound to discover errors that were not exposed during testing and debugging, no matter how rigorous the testing. "What we can test," Davis said, "is the match between the program and the specification, which is not at all the same thing as the specifications and what the world is."

Software development is often likened to architecture, another design-intensive activity. Kapor noted that both activities are devoted to accommodating human needs and motivations, as well as to satisfying aesthetic tastes. Davis pointed to a fundamental difference, however. Software does not have a physical embodiment that can be represented pictorially, as in blueprints or architectural diagrams. Details often cannot be pinned down in advance. "There is almost no way to visualize software," Davis explained. "Sure, we have flow charts, we have data-flow diagrams, we have control-flow diagrams, and everybody knows how basically useless those are. Flow charts are documentation you write afterward—because management requires them, not because they are a useful tool."

## BOX 3.1—CONSTANT ITERATION: STEPS IN
## DEVELOPING SOFTWARE*

*Specify the problem and define the constraints.*
The process begins with a general description of the intended application, which then must be evaluated and reevaluated in light of such constraints as memory requirements, speed of execution, ease of use, and desired completion date.

*Design externals.*
Determine how the program will interact with the outside world—users, input devices, other programs, output devices. Will the program inputs, for example, be entered by keyboard or voice commands? How will data on disk files be handled?

*Design internals.*
Set up the data structure, organize movement and processing of the data, and identify the critical points of data control, as well as the languages and algorithms to be used.

*Transform the design into code.*
Use own existing code or license it from others, when feasible; write new code. Assemble these elements into a prototype program for testing. Respecify the problem on the basis of new understanding, and change the design accordingly.

*Test, retest, and test again.*
Evaluate the prototype's performance with real users and real data. Identify bugs and performance trade-offs. As needed, change the code, design, constraints, and problem description.

*Document for the user.*
Explain how to use the program, how it works, and how to modify it. Change the program to improve the documentation, if necessary.

*Package and market.*
Adapt the product, if necessary, to fit the distribution medium, such as a floppy disk or compact disk. Prepare manuals. Advertise and position the product in the market. Change the product to accommodate new hardware or to adjust to new market conditions.

*Support the product.*
As appropriate, create user groups and provide on-site training, telephone help lines, and informational publications. Track user feedback, correct bugs, identify incompatibilities, and begin evaluating features to include in the next product version.

*Abstracted from a talk given by Dan Bricklin, Software Garden, Inc., at CSTB's December 1989 forum.

Taken together, two attributes ascribed to software—the uniqueness of each product and the incremental, additive nature of the development process—appear to be contradictory. "You use code that worked before—bags of tricks," Bricklin explained. "You license code from others or use stuff that is built into the operating system . . . . You write new code. You tie it all together with all sorts of different types of glue."

If the code underlying a specific function, such as methods for searching databases, can be used in many applications, then where does the uniqueness, or originality, in a product lie? Often, Bricklin and others maintained, reusable components require very specific tailoring to be incorporated into new applications. If cars were built in the same manner, Davis explained, the size of each screw used in their construction would be different.

More important, however, is the composite nature of the product. "Most software is an accretion of pieces of software that have been previously developed, used in ways the original innovator never contemplated," explained Francis Fisher, adviser to the Educational Technology Group at the Harvard Law School. "This reassembling of bits and pieces is greatly in the public interest. That is how software progresses."

Thus each new development project begins at a "higher jumping-off point," Kapor added, "because there are more layers" to integrate. "But once you actually sit down to write your piece, your program, it is still grinding code, and testing and debugging."

This peculiarity of software poses a quandary for intellectual property law. A large number of companies are in the business of producing reusable software components. This market illustrates the problem of balance: on the one hand, overly rigid protections could undermine a slowly growing foundation of reusable components. On the other hand, without intellectual property protections, these companies could not exist. Although those in the field disagree on the depth and breadth of the foundation, software developers would like to exploit whatever experience is accumulating. "You have to be careful about protecting [code] that can be used all over the place—very careful," Bricklin warned. The law, he added, should encourage developers to pursue successively higher levels of innovation, but without preventing them from exploring and implementing new iterations of existing ideas and methods. If protection confers monopoly at too high a level in Bricklin's tree-like scheme of software innovation, access to branches leading to new designs and applications would be blocked, he said.

## SOFTWARE AS A CREATIVE MEDIUM

At its most abstract, software is "the ultimate creative medium," said MIT's Davis. It is, according to Davis, "a tangible form of dreams and imagination."

Yet in software, abstraction and metaphor are embodied within the product. The popularity of Apple's Macintosh computer, for example, is attributed to a graphical user interface that mimics the desktop work environment—in visual imagery, in the behavior of the file folders, trash cans, and other objects depicted on the screen, and in the interaction between the user and these objects. Indeed, a major aim of software development is to create user interfaces in which "electronic reality and actual reality completely overlap and reinforce each other," said Bruce Tognazzini, who started the human interface group at Apple Computer. Thus software seeks to simulate reality and to achieve cognitive compatibility with computer users, a combination of features that, many software designers maintain, distinguishes it from other technologies.

Reichman of Vanderbilt disagreed with this claim. Industrial designers, he suggested during the forum, would argue that software design is merely one application of advanced techniques that are routinely applied to other innovative products.

Another hallmark of software is its malleability as a creative tool and, consequently, its nearly unlimited utility. In a technical sense, said MIT's Davis, "software is the universal machine. . . . We can really do anything with the machine, and as a consequence, we, in fact, try to do everything with it." The results are products that enable a computer user to perform given tasks, not unlike, as Kapor pointed out, conventional machines made of iron, steel, or plastic. Yet, for the purposes of copyright law, software is treated as analogous to a literary work.

Several software attributes, according to Kapor, strain the analogy to literary works. Books and other works on paper, he said, are fixed in form, sequential, noninteractive, uncoupled from the real world, and nonfunctional in the sense of performing work. In contrast, software is a dynamic composite—an assembly of many different programs—that, unlike pages in a book, can change its working order at the beckoning of the user. Software, therefore, has a chameleon-like identity, as "literary expression that does useful work," Kapor said. He added, however, that identity cannot be ascribed on the basis of function, because the tasks performed by a particular piece of software are invoked at the direction of the user.

Because of software's underlying fluidity, however, definitional schemes can quickly become meaningless, Esther Dyson cautioned. For example, she said, the popular spreadsheet program Lotus 1-2-3 was initially viewed as a user application for performing accounting operations. But users have discovered the broader utility of the software. "It isn't just interactive; it's a creative tool. If you perform a sequence of actions in 1-2-3," she explained, "you may end up creating [a new] application. You define the sequence of application actions, give it a name—call it a macro—and you are suddenly using an application as a language, and you have created—potentially—a new piece of intellectual property within the old one.

"So, the stuff is very fluid. You can't say this is an application; this is a language." Therefore, she said, "[Y]ou don't want to make rules that apply to applications versus language versus interfaces without understanding that in the end these might be the very same things."

Similarly, particular functions can be embodied in either software or hardware, and "in most cases the preferred embodiment will change over time," said John Shoch, general partner at the Asset Management Co. Still, each advance in hardware has the direct effect of expanding the role of software.

Because of this continuing evolution, Harry Reinstein of Aion prefers to conceptualize software as componentry incorporated into a never-finished product. He suggested that very few software products, even the largest ones, are fully independent entities. "We no longer build complete systems. . .," Reinstein said. "We build components that must, to be useful, work with other components, and that is why the issue of interfaces is absolutely critical to this industry." Restricting access to software components, he maintained, would suppress innovation, hamper the entry of new firms into the industry, and limit the utility of software. Again, the issue is one of balance. Protections should prohibit copying of components, he said, but they should not dampen competitive activity that builds on existing software to develop new applications.

## THE INFLUENCE OF THE MARKET

Although they confer ownership rights that vary in nature, copyrights, patents, and trade secrets are, in part, measures that help ensure the lead-time advantage. Exclusivity, however, carries a risk, especially if it results in a product whose functionality is isolated from that of other offerings on the market. Interoperability, achieved by licensing or by allowing the free use of program-to-program interfaces, protocols, languages, and other types of interfaces, can enhance the value of an individual software offering. It increases utility for computer owners who may use the products of several vendors and who, for example, may want one program to generate data that will be processed by another application. In contrast, a product that is an entity unto itself limits user choices and, consequently, restricts the size of the product's potential market.

Therefore the marketplace sometimes provides incentives that counterbalance inclinations to be overly protective and to regard all "home-grown" innovations as proprietary. A firm that deems an interface as proprietary to safeguard against the copying of the application behind the interface may be making a tactical business error. Instead of protecting the "corporate jewels," said Scott G. Davis, senior consulting engineer at the Digital Equipment Corp., a proprietary stance on interfaces may be "protecting the corporate fool's gold." Yet, understandably, the more money, time, and personnel a firm has devoted to developing an interface, or the more effectively it has established a dominant market position, the stronger its urge to protect the interface for exclusive use.

In common with other industries, the software industry can find especially precarious the footing on the tightrope between the need to guard proprietary interests and the desire to cultivate a large product market. In the software industry, however, the lack of common understanding of what constitutes an interface can escalate "normal" problems of contract interpretation when firms disagree on whether an interface is open or on the nature of the rights of use accorded in licensing contracts. In the view of some industry observers, firms have promoted widespread use of particular innovations to cultivate the market for their commercial implementations, but then have reversed themselves by declaring the innovations proprietary and demanding royalties for their use. These and other misunderstandings arise, according to a position paper issued by the Association of Data Processing Service Organizations (ADAPSO), because of "assumptions that are founded on differing views regarding the extent of intellectual property claims."

## SYMBIOSIS IN THE MARKET

In the personal computer side of the software industry, the competitive environment has given rise to a new form of business behavior that, according to Kapor of ON Technology, should not be jeopardized by legal concerns. When Apple and then IBM disclosed the architectures of their personal computers, they provided independent software developers with the opportunity to write applications for the machines without entering into a contractual relationship with the manufacturers. Thousands of software applications were written by third-party developers, motivated by the prospect of market success. In turn, those who succeeded by writing high-quality programs benefited the hardware manufacturers by increasing the utility and value of their computers.

"The economic cost of trying to achieve the same result—if each and every relationship between the software company and hardware company had had to be negotiated—would have been so high that, as a practical matter, it would have been completely impossible," Kapor said. All of this innovative, value-adding activity, he added, is mediated through open interfaces, creating a "new industrial ecology." This style of business relationship—Kapor calls it a "nonrelationship relationship"—is a "very good way for pushing the whole system forward."

This symbiosis is also reflected in the composition of personal-computer software. "If you are running an application . . .," Kapor explained, "you are actually using software that is made by about four or five different companies, each of which is calling the other's interface." But as in all segments of the industry, developers of applications for personal computers are becoming increasingly aware of the risk of copyright and patent infringement, which could undermine this form of business relationship and reduce the flow of benefits it generates for users.

## THE CASE OF INTERFACES

From single routines to large compilations of many programs, elements of software owe their value to their role in some larger system. Within a single program, for example, individual routines are interdependent, each one's task shaped by the functions performed by others. In software systems, interdependency is magnified, as the number of interacting entities multiplies to include many different users, many different pieces of hardware, and many different programs, remote and internal.

Interfaces account for much of the utility and behavior—the value—of software and hardware. Points of interaction between otherwise independent components, interfaces link machine to machine, software to machine, application to application, and user to computer. As the complexity of hardware and software has grown and as the push for interoperability has gained momentum, the number of interfaces of all types has multiplied, as have questions about the appropriateness of available intellectual property protections.

By design, external interfaces (as opposed to internal interfaces that interconnect modules within a single software product) facilitate cooperation with the outside world. From the perspective of users, more cooperation, or compatibility, translates into greater value by enhancing the capability of computers and by expanding access to the software offerings of many different vendors. For vendors that have invested in defining interfaces between proprietary applications, evolving compatibility poses a quandary. Software interfaces are often the product of significant investment, creative activity, and engineering effort. To make an interface public is to share the fruits of this work with the entire industry. And to the extent that functions are bound up within an interface, they become vulnerable to copying. However, companies that designate an interface as proprietary run the risk of restricting the size of the market for their products.

The debate over proprietary interests in program code that expresses external interfaces is intense and often divides the industry. Those firms offering integrated systems solutions to computer communications environments see component interfaces as crucial elements of proprietary value added. Those who produce software and hardware components that must attach to and work with complex information systems see proprietary interfaces as a barrier to market entry. Thus, even if intellectual property law provides reasonable protection for interfaces—the subject of a wide spectrum of opinion—business strategies dictate whether a firm will deem an interface as open or proprietary.

Complicating the situation is the slippery identity of the various classes of interfaces (see Box 3.2). Peter Schneider, IBM's vice president for systems and programming, joked that interfaces are as difficult to define as pornography. "We all know what an interface is," he said, "but none of us will have the same definition." What to the original designer is a self-contained subroutine—and not an interface—may be a convenient point of attachment to the designer of another product, who may also want to exploit some of the functions performed by the original.

The issue of whether a specific interface should be viewed as proprietary or, because of its utility to users, as open and appropriate for public use has many facets. For example, computer languages function as interfaces in that they are used to interpret electronic input and to formulate messages that direct a computer to carry out a sequence of actions. Obviously, languages have great utility, but opinion is divided on whether they can be protected by copyright law. A related issue concerns the protectability of specific language phrases, or sequences of keystrokes, that direct a computer to perform a specific function.[1] For users, copyrighting of keystroke sequences might mean

---

### BOX 3.2—INTERFACES AND SPECIFICATIONS

An interface is the boundary between two environments. An interface specification describes what happens on the "other side" of the interface when certain specified information is moved through the interface; the specification also describes what the responses might be to the environment from which the stimulus came.

The specification of a human interface might tell you what the meaning is of what you see on a screen and what will happen when certain actions are taken. The specification might also describe the kinds of information that can be dispatched from the environment on the other side of the interface. Similarly, the specification of a networking interface might describe the format of messages required for sending and receiving information through the interface.

The key is the specification of the form of information that crosses an interface, plus a description of the meaning of the information crossing the interface. The specification says nothing about implementation, only information and behavior.

—Scott G. Davis, Senior Consulting Engineer, Digital Equipment Corp.

---

that commands for the same function will vary from program to program.

Issues such as these, said Ingari of Lotus, have made interfaces "one of the nastiest and most difficult areas" for the software industry to reckon with. And nowhere do the issues become more problematic and more contentious than in the visual and behavioral domain where machine and human interact, the user interface. Increasingly, the "look and feel" of the user interface is becoming the definitive attribute of software: the more intuitive an application's method of operation and the more appealing and the more informative its graphical display, then the better the working relationship between user and software and the more powerful a tool the computer becomes.

User interfaces are also emerging as the primary asset of firms that specialize in software development and of those that offer entire information systems. "Increasingly, the economic value is absolutely inseparable from that part of the program that the user directly interacts with and experiences," Kapor said.

Debate over what is and what is not protectable in user interfaces has spawned a rash of "look and feel" lawsuits. The central challenge to judges in these cases (who will vary in their technical sophistication) is distinguishing the elements of interfaces that are protectable expressions from their underlying ideas, which should reside in the public domain. But some software designers doubt whether the distinction can be made.

"There is something funny about interfaces in which idea is bound with expression," Aion's Reinstein said. Added Kapor, "The problem is that our traditional distinctions between idea and expression, as far as I can tell, always wind up tripping all over themselves when it comes to software." And in user interfaces all of the peculiarities of software as a technological entity are magnified.

The sections that follow provide a brief overview of the evolution of user interfaces and discuss some of the factors that underlie innovation in this important area of software.

### Evolution of User Interfaces

User interfaces have been called the last frontier in software design (Foley, 1987). As they improve, so does our adroitness in wielding the computer as a tool. Simply put, each generation of improvements in the graphical display and the behavior of programs has made computers easier to use.

These advances stem from the ability of designers, artists, and engineers to encapsulate useful metaphors in electronic form. Perhaps today's best known metaphor-based interface is the desktop, as embodied in Apple's Macintosh computer and in several other systems. Another successful interface is the electronic spreadsheet's two-dimensional field of rows and columns and its internal logic that meshes with the user's natural way of thinking and working.

Both examples demonstrate the benefits that result when appearance and behavior are successfully mated in a well-designed interface. The first electronic displays, in contrast, did not achieve this match. According to Apple's Tognazzini, these early interfaces resembled mechanical teletype machines, but with an important difference that frustrated more than a few users. "Things came 'kerchunking' up from the bottom of the display," he recalled, "and eventually kerchunked off into infinity at the top of the display forever. . . . When somebody wrote a routine that would allow you to scroll downwards, we were all blown away. By slavishly adhering to a limited metaphor, the original designers had lost a new power that an electronic display could have provided—namely, downward review and scrolling."

Although today's interfaces mark a significant advance over the "Stone Age" of interactive computing, they too will be deemed primitive by the standards of the not-too-distant future. The most ambitious developmental efforts seek to create artificial, or virtual, realities, three-dimensional renderings that simulate actual environments and are responsive not only to keyboard commands, but also to speech, touch, and even eye contact. Advanced flight simulators, which produce the imagery and "orchestrate the sound, force, and motion that approximate the aerodynamic behavior of an airborne plane" (Foley, 1987, p. 127), serve as an example. Industry visionaries predict advances that will enable personal computer users to make their own animated movies and, in essence, their own artificial realities. "So, 'you ain't seen nuthin' yet,'" said Tognazzini.

## Where Does Innovation Lie?

While creativity, superior design, and sweat-of-the-brow programming effort underlie all good software , high-quality user interfaces may rank as the superlative example. An embodiment of art, human intuition, and elements of various science and engineering disciplines, interfaces are the products of a process that stands out because of the intensiveness and complexity of the design effort required to produce what some call "aesthetic functionality."

Compared with software applications alone, said Spinrad of Xerox, "there is a different kind of invention and a different kind of creativity required" to develop a user interface that complements the way people think. Interface designers, he continued, must have the skills of cognitive scientists and a "gut understanding of what you can or cannot achieve computationally."

Tognazzini characterized interface designers as illusionists who, unconstrained by their medium, create their own natural laws. The goal, he said, is to "create an illusion that doesn't break down." That is, the behavior and the visual appearance of the objects in the illusion created on a computer screen, be it a spreadsheet display or a flight simulation, must mesh perceptually with all applications that use the interface. "There is a paradox," Tognazzini said. "The simpler the system that you sit down to use, probably the more complex the design process that went into it. The more obvious the feature, the more difficult or creative it was to generate that feature. For example, pull-down menus and overlapping windows seem like obvious solutions, but they required years and years of careful experimentation and playing before we hit upon them."

Iteration, experimentation, and research on user behavior and psychology are involved in the selection of graphical symbols that best represent functions, objects, or ideas on the screen, according to Ingari of Lotus, who likened the process to the evolution of written language from hieroglyphic figures. But efforts devoted to achieving a visual connection with the user constitute only one element of the process. In tandem, the design team must also work on the "back side" of the interface, conceiving, structuring, and implementing the data structures and other software layers that underlie the behavior of the interface and complete the cognitive link to the user. If successful, the development effort results in an organic work, a merger of form and function.

"The original version of [Lotus] 1-2-3 and its interface required a great deal of hard work—hundreds of hours, multiple iterations," explained Kapor, co-developer of the popular spreadsheet program. "It was very nonobvious, and it was tested on users . . . . It would certainly require a lot less effort to design a spreadsheet that used the same menu tree because you wouldn't have to go through that."

Ingari maintained that understanding the complexity of the design and development process will give a "very clear sense of the difference between the pieces of interfaces that should be and will be in the public sphere and the pieces of the interface that must be protected because they represent the essence of the work that is done to create value." But others were less certain that the innovation within a user interface can be dissected from the entirety of the work. "We have this problem," said Davis of MIT, "that the innovation is the expression, is the value, and they become inseparable."

Under copyright law, however, some courts have split user interfaces into two components—the screen display, which is viewed as a pictorial or an audiovisual work, and the underlying program, which is deemed a literary work. Even though they are embodied in a single technical product, the two copyright categories are accorded different rights under the law, explained Goldstein of the Stanford Law School. The Copyright Office has taken the position that ". . . all copyrightable expression owned by the same claimant and embodied in a computer program, or first published as a unit with a computer program, including computer screen displays, is considered a single work and should be registered on a single application form."

To Kapor, this legal parsing ignores the "organicity" of the user interface, akin to describing the human senses of touch, vision, and speech without recognizing the role of the brain. The user interface—both its appearance and its behavior—"is not separable from the program. It has roots potentially in every single line of code, in every algorithm . . . ." Yet, said Reichman, "A merger of form and function is precisely why copyright laws everywhere tend to reject industrial designs. In the United States, this rejection is accomplished by a doctrine of separability that was applied to industrial art, but not to industrial literature. This distinction is totally incoherent and ultimately indefensible."

The unitary nature of user interfaces notwithstanding, the issues at the heart of pending "look and feel" suits entail disentangling the innovative elements of products from those elements that do not merit protection because, for example, they are more appropriately viewed as ideas or they do not reach the legal threshold for originality. For now, these issues seem to lack conceptual clarity. Yet, as Dyson explained, resolving the legal ferment that surrounds software in general and user interfaces in particular requires assigning value to the elements or combination of elements spawned by creativity and superior engineering. "This," she said, "is what we want to provide incentives for."

## SUMMARY

Is software a special case, different from other technologies in the ways it is designed, made, and used? Or, as Reichman contended, is it another subset of advanced industrial design whose uncertain status in systems of intellectual property law has never been effectively addressed?

Software's characteristics—both positive and negative—are relevant to assessments of the adequacy of intellectual property protections for the technology. Some familiarity with the distinguishing features of software is essential for assessing how well law and technology mesh. Likewise, appreciation for the process of creating software— from idea to marketable product—aids understanding of how the law can foster or hinder innovation.

## NOTE

1. The *Lotus Development Corporation v. Paperback Software International and Stephenson Software, Limited* (Civil Action No. 87-76-K, U.S. District Court for the District of Massachusetts, 740 F. Supp. 37 [June 28, 1990]) case addressed this issue at length.

Even the possibility that the legal basis for a stable, functional marketplace for computer software might be threatened is enough to create alarm in the industry, . . . one of the few high-tech industries in which U.S. firms still enjoy a commanding position in international trade.

—Lewis Branscomb, *Director, Science, Technology and Public Policy Program, Harvard University*

As an attorney, I want to make it possible for him [the businessman] to be able to get back something on the R&D investment, which today can run millions and millions of dollars.

—J. Jancin, Jr., *Counsel, IBM Corp.*

The purpose of the Constitution is to protect originality and useful originality. So, if you spend $3 billion doing something fundamentally useless, the Constitution doesn't really care.

—Esther Dyson, *Publisher, "Release 1.0"*

[T]here is a stultifying, dulling effect—in some cases subtle, [in others] not so subtle—[resulting from] the confusion that has arisen in this field, which is slowing down activity. It is slowing down the small companies, . . . and it is slowing down the large companies.

—Robert Spinrad, *Director, Corporate Technology, Xerox Corp.*

Copyright is procompetitive. It allows the competitor to enter a market by independently creating, via his own R&D, a competing product.

—Howard G. Figueroa, *Vice President, Commercial and Industry Relations, IBM Corp.*

We can be hurt in our company by too much protection or too little protection.

—Frank Ingari, *Vice President, Spreadsheet Division, Lotus Development Corp.*

# 4

# A Closer Look at Current Issues

Legal uncertainty can take many forms: Is a particular software element "prior art" and thus freely available, or is it wending its way through the patent process, emerging months from now as exclusively owned intellectual property? What protection—patent or copyright—is most appropriate for a particular innovation? Will either one provide adequate protection, or should the innovation remain a trade secret? Is the specification of a software application an idea or is it expression? What constitutes "comprehensive nonliteral similarity"? Is the goal of compatibility a legally valid argument for adopting others' ideas and even parts of their implementation? This litany of questions could go on and on. The lack of clear answers to most underlies the "stultifying, dulling effect" that Xerox's Robert Spinrad complained intellectual property concerns are imposing on the industry.

Because so many questions are unresolved, according to Francis Fisher, adviser to the Harvard Law School's Educational Technology Group, the software industry often cannot predict how intellectual property law applies to specific types of behavior shown by firms in the marketplace, to concerns about specific elements of software, or industry-wide issues, such as compatibility and interoperability. As a result, Fisher said, developers are forced to "gamble on unpredictable judicial interpretation."

While the hope is that decisions in pending litigation and in cases yet to come will eventually yield predictable guides, another outcome might be inconsistent decisions, which could generate in their aftermath greater uncertainty and more law suits. A single decision can have far-reaching effects, perhaps changing the behavior of the entire industry, and a hasty search for legislative remedies would likely ensue, advised Michael J. Remington, chief counsel for the Subcommittee on Intellectual Property in the U.S. House of Representatives. "If disaster strikes," he said, "bills will be introduced in the Congress that will not be thought through, and we may end up with another statutory scheme that we may live to regret in the long run."

This scenario is, of course, speculative. Indeed, one could argue, as did Howard G. Figueroa, IBM Corp. vice president for commercial and industrial relations, that such speculation should not obscure evidence indicating that the software industry has prospered under the current intellectual property system. Statistical measures show, he said, that the software industry is an increasingly important segment of the U.S. economy, contributing as a "wealth producer and as a trade-balance enhancer."

"Industry-wide in the United States," Figueroa added, "the copyright system has worked well, inspiring the authorship of original programs" and engendering "head-on competition."

Yet another perspective suggests it is precisely because of the industry's strong performance, as well as because of the growing utility and value of software, that today's legal issues are regarded with urgency by many. "Even the possibility that the legal basis for a stable, functional marketplace is threatened," noted Lewis Branscomb of Harvard University, "is enough to create alarm in the industry, . . . one of the few high-tech industries in which U.S. firms still enjoy a commanding position in international trade."

Point and counterpoint largely characterize discussions of the adequacy of intellectual property protection. In the remainder of this chapter, some of the issues fueling this debate are examined in more detail.

## PROTECTED OR UNPROTECTED?

The software industry consists of followers and leaders. The most innovative firms open new product areas, creating applications that add new dimensions of utility and value to computers. Follower firms, recognizing the opportunity to increase revenues by moving into a new market, respond to commercially promising innovation by developing products that embody variations of the original inventor's idea. Sometimes the products of follower firms are better embodiments of the idea—superior, perhaps, in performance and function or lower in price—than those of the pioneering firm. Occasionally, a follower might introduce a product that is a "knock off" of the original, a mere copy that might be altered to avoid the suspicion of duplication.

Between the extremes of "knock offs" and products that are the result of major leaps in innovation is a vast middle ground where some of the most difficult business and legal decisions lie. As discussed in chapter 3, software designers and programmers often use techniques, data structures, algorithms, and even lines of code developed by others, but for entirely different applications. Some of these bits and pieces reside in the public domain or, in the terms of patent law, would be recognized as *prior art*. But the status of other borrowed elements may not be clear. Software designer Dan Bricklin noted that designers may use elements that they believe are prior art only to find later that those elements have been patented. The designers may prevail in an infringement case, but the cost of pursuing those objections in court can be prohibitive.

Frank Ingari, who oversees software development in Lotus's Spreadsheet Division, described the dilemma. He said he has "concerns on both sides of protection, as in, 'Are my guys using something they shouldn't be using?' which I have to worry about as much as the other side of the discussion—'Am I protecting what I am developing?'"

Often the answers to these questions are not clear because of grey areas in intellectual property law. Under patent law's doctrine of equivalents or copyright law's concept of substantial similarity, for example, an independently developed and arguably dissimilar software component might be deemed similar enough to constitute infringement. Thus far, developers have little guidance to help them assess, before investing creative effort and financial resources, the likelihood of such an outcome.

Without adequate direction on the scope, durability, and application of patent and copyright protections, firms may operate on the presumption that their products and innovations are vulnerable to theft by a competitor. The tendency may be to rely on trade secrets, and the result, warned Esther Dyson, will be a "world of stagnation. Remember, too, we're talking not just about vendors, but about users creating and either sharing or hiding valuable technology. Without an assumption of protection, we probably won't have, say, shared airline reservation systems, efficient money markets, and so forth." Whether lack of sharing and interaction will occur is yet to be seen; in some aspects of the market, a steadily increasing proportion of software sales has been of non-trade secret software.

One indication that firms are either wary or uninformed of the protection accorded by patents and copyrights can be seen in the results of a survey sponsored by the Massachusetts Software Council.[1] About 75 percent of the respondents said that they relied on trade secret law, and only 25 percent relied on copyright, even though this latter protection applies to works of authorship, published and unpublished, and can be used in conjunction with trade secrets. Only 8 percent of the software vendors said they used patents. Heavy reliance on trade secret law can pose considerable risk since innovations protected in this manner do not qualify as prior art and, therefore, may be eligible for patenting, perhaps by a competing firm.

## THE PATENT-COPYRIGHT INTERFACE

If for no other reason, the status of software as both patentable and copyrightable intellectual property makes the technology unusual. As has long been true of some industrial designs in developed countries, explained Jerome Reichman of Vanderbilt University, treatment in both legal domains poses the potential for a conflict between two conceptually separate branches of the law—copyright and patent—at both the domestic and the international levels. Stressing the need for a "holistic approach" to the different forms of intellectual property protection, John Shoch of the Asset Management Co. said that the seeming division of legal perspectives frustrates those within the industry. "[W]e can have a wonderful discourse on the impact and limits of copyright law," he said, "and we can have another wonderful discourse on the limits of patent law, and it is right at the edge where things get interesting." Treatises on copyright, Shoch added, focus on distinguishing between protectable expression and idea, the point at which patent lawyers are likely "to pick up the gauntlet."

Yet software seems amenable to both protections, sometimes simultaneously. For example, copyright attorneys can argue cogently that disputes over the ownership of graphical displays and the sequencing of commands—that is, the look and feel of user interfaces—should be resolved in the copyright arena because the issues center on creative expression. Objecting to the subjectivity of copyright concepts, such as "look and feel" and "structure, sequence, and organization," patent attorneys argue just as persuasively that the issues can be addressed more concretely by assessing the novelty and nonobviousness of useful processes incorporated into interfaces.

A major challenge, according to Branscomb of Harvard University, is to differentiate between the "elements of the technology that seem to take you, on the one hand, to copyright and, on the other hand, to patent." Moreover, some elements seem to be "inexorably linked" to both laws, "so that you have to figure out a way to invoke both sets of principles," he said.

## PATENT PROBLEMS: STRUCTURAL OR LEGAL?

Even the most ardent advocates of patent protection for software find the current patent system to be deficient in some structural and administrative areas. Those who question the appropriateness of patents for software-related inventions include these shortcomings in their appraisals, but only as a starting point that leads to more fundamental concerns.

University of Washington law professor Donald Chisum, a strong proponent of patents for software, listed six problems in the procurement and enforcement of patents, none of them peculiar to software. The first is the expense of searching for previously patented inventions as a precautionary step to avoid infringement and then of preparing, filing, negotiating, and maintaining a patent. Estimates of these costs range from about $15,000 to more than $25,000 (Kahin, 1989). Second is the length of the patent review and approval process, averaging about 30 months, or nearly a year longer than the average for other inventions. During this period, the patent application remains confidential, undisclosed to other inventors who may also wish to patent a similar innovation. Except for the United States, said Chisum, every industrial nation "has a procedure for publishing patent applications 18 months after they are filed." He added, however, that firms compound the delay by waiting too long before applying for a patent.

The third problem Chisum cited is "inadequate examination by the Patent and Trademark Office," contributing to delays and the issuance of patents for ambiguous claims. Additional training for patent examiners and creation of advisory boards composed of representatives from industry and academia could remedy this deficiency, he suggested. Imprecise claims, at the heart of Chisum's fourth concern, ambiguity in the scope of issued patents, in turn spawn lawsuits. Chisum said these can constitute a fifth problem, "arguably groundless suits, in some instances financed either by attorneys on a contingency-fee basis or by simply going out and openly raising money from investors to speculate on the outcome of a patent suit against a major company." Completing his list of shortcomings, Chisum noted that patent enforcement is country specific, a problem for companies selling products in international markets. Not only must firms seek patents in each nation where they sell their product, but they also must conform to procedures and requirements that vary among countries. For software firms this variability is especially problematic, because not all nations extend patent protection to software.

While Chisum sees these problems as affecting all technologies, others view the consequences as more severe for software. An overriding concern is the danger of being blindsided—of pursuing an innovation that may already be patented or that may be in the patent-review pipeline. The first difficulty, according to Dyson, publisher of "Release 1.0," could be assuaged with a "meaningful, automatically updating electronic database that contains information on patented technologies." Currently, searches of patent literature are error-prone exercises, incurring a high risk of overlooking relevant subject matter because of the fragmented, disorganized state of patent information. The second issue, that of losing out to a competitor whose application was submitted earlier, is more problematic because of the short life cycle of software products. Thus the competitor who loses out on a patent has the option of licensing the innovation from the patent holder, if that option exists, or of foregoing the next generation of the product-development cycle.

Eventually, claims Brian Kahin, the rapid rate of innovation in the software industry will be slowed to conform with the pace of the patent review and approval process. More worrisome to Kahin and others are the combined effects of the approval of overly broad claims and the scope of patent protection. Software innovator Bricklin, creator of the original spreadsheet program, VisiCalc, believes that the combination could be "very bad for the industry," antithetical to the industry's propensity for "frequent independent innovation." Had patents been available when he and his collaborator developed Visi-Calc, Bricklin speculated, their company, Software Arts, would have sought the protection. The consequences of such a decision, he further speculated, would have been to prevent other innovators from exploring different expressions of the spreadsheet idea and to handicap the competition, blocking the development of today's successful spreadsheet programs, such as Excel and Lotus 1-2-3. The consequence of foregoing a patent in this hypothetical situation, however, would be to eliminate a sizable source of revenues. "There are not many," Chisum said, "who will say, 'I knew I could get a patent worth $200 million, but I think I will pass it up this time'"; in fact, Chisum added, the potential for such a loss strikes fear in the heart of most companies and should motivate them to file for patents promptly, thereby resulting in timely disclosure and hastening the pace of development.

Several forum participants were unwilling to dismiss the awarding of patents for overly broad claims as simply a structural problem that will diminish as the Patent Office becomes more experienced with software-related inventions and as rulings by the District Courts and Court of Appeals for the Federal Circuit (CAFC) clarify issues pertaining to the patenting of software. To them, such patents have the potential to inflict long-term damage if they are upheld by the courts.

The evidence, though limited and often circumstantial, suggests that the courts will look favorably on at least some of these claims. For example, in a case cited by Fisher (*Magnavox Co. v. Activision, Inc.*, 848 F.2d 1244 [Fed. Cir. 1988]), the courts held that Activision, the maker of a video game in which an animated track runner fails to clear a hurdle and knocks it down, infringed on a patent (licensed exclusively to Magnavox) on the idea in software of having one object hit another, causing it to move.

Patents have been granted for products or software-directed processes that some believe do not satisfy the patent law's criterion of nonobviousness, either because they are too abstract or are merely descriptions of ideas that are already in the public domain. Such objections have been raised over patents issued for footnoting, redlining (text comparison), merging of documents, and other processes. Extrapolating from these instances, Kahin anticipates that patents will eventually be awarded for automated methods of performing common business practices and for interactive learning techniques. It remains to be seen, however, whether the courts will uphold patents based on broad claims. As a rule of thumb, patent attorneys estimate that the CAFC, which has jurisdiction over appeals of patent decisions made by the District Courts, upholds about half of all patents. Even if the courts do find an ambiguous software patent to be valid, however, it is not certain whether they will rule that a competitor's specific implementation of ideas expressed in a patent constitutes infringement.

To Mitchell Kapor of ON Technology, this wait-and-see attitude is unsatisfactory, inserting more uncertainty into an already uncertain legal situation. Waiting for rulings on the validity of broad claims, he said, creates a situation akin to the "greenhouse effect," the controversial projection of global warming due to growing atmospheric concentrations of carbon dioxide and other heat-absorbing gases. "The sense that I have now," Kapor said, acknowledging opinions to the contrary, "is that we face, potentially, some disasters from inappropriate software patents."

If the software industry's "greenhouse effect is real," he continued, "then we have a very, very, very serious problem, disrupting the activities of large and small companies. [D]oing nothing and letting matters work themselves out in the courts seem to be unwise." At this stage, according to Chisum, only a few general trends that have unfolded under the relatively recent influence of software-related patents are discernible. "We will see more procuring of patents," he said. "We will see more licensing and then eventually litigation."

Chisum's scenario is suggestive of conditions that already exist in the hardware industry, where patents and licensing are a regular part of doing business. Most manufacturers of computer hardware maintain a portfolio of patents, which are cross-licensed with the portfolios of major competitors. Typically, a manufacturer will require access to other firms' innovations to make a product, and yet that same manufacturer will hold patents essential to competitors' products. In making an integrated circuit, for example, a semiconductor manufacturer may use technologies patented by 20 companies. Because of this interdependency, patents on hardware only occasionally impede the product-development efforts of established firms. But start-up firms, lacking a patent portfolio of sufficient size and, therefore, the associated leverage for bargaining with competitors, are likely to be at a disadvantage.[2]

If patenting becomes as pervasive in software as it is in hardware, Kahin predicts that the software industry will undergo rapid consolidation. "Although cross-licensing allows efficient, competitive exploitation of patents in industries where there are relatively few firms of roughly similar size," he has written, "cross-licensing will not work for the many thousands of small firms and tens of thousands of individuals in the software industry, because these small players have little or nothing to bring to the table. The vision of cross-licensing as a solution to the problem of software patents implicitly assumes a whole-sale shakeout and restructuring of the industry" (Kahin, 1989, pp. 9-10).

Not all small software producers agree with this prognosis. Indeed, presidents of six California-based software firms painted quite a different picture in a letter to the *New York Times*: "By making an invention the temporary property of its inventor, patents become the lifeblood of small innovative technology companies. It [patents] lets them attract investors and gives incentive to improve the property, educate the market, and market the product. Without patents, an entrenched competitor can merely wait for others to innovate and incorporate innovations into its products only when inventions are proved and market share is threatened" (Gasper et al., 1989).

## COMPATIBILITY AND INTEROPERABILITY

While it is clear that the public interest is served by industry behavior that yields a wide variety of high-quality, reasonably priced software, it is also clear that consumers want to be freed of the constraints of incompatible proprietary systems, which prevent them from realizing the full fruits of the diversity of software offerings. After purchasing a vendor's system, users often discover that a particular set of needs would be best served by applications designed to run on another proprietary system. Precisely because of this variability in the utility and quality of software applications, organizations may purchase hardware from several different vendors. Incompatibilities, however, prevent users from exchanging the results of applications between unlike machines or from using the same graphical display on different machines or with different software—unless they make a hefty investment in systems integration.

Underlying the crescendo of user demand for compatibility is a facet of software use that, apart from its technological and design underpinnings, distinguishes it from other media, such as paintings and literary works. Once they become accustomed to the look and feel of an interface, users would rather stick with the same interface than use a different one for each new application. For works of art, in contrast, such imitation would be regarded as offensive, as well as make for dull art museums. In addition, Aion's Harry Reinstein pointed out that once users have selected a computer operating system or a database management system, they are, by analogy, committing themselves to one artistic genre, a specific user interface.

A parallel situation in book buying was hypothesized by Reinstein. "If I buy a mystery story," he said, "I will forever limit myself to buying mystery stories with that set of characters, that major detective, and, therefore, presumably that author. That is exactly the situation in which we find ourselves in commercial software. By and large, if you buy an operating system you don't trivially change it."

Demand for interoperability arises from the usefulness, or machine-like nature, of software, rather than its aesthetics. For machines, compatibility is a well-recognized virtue. "It is in the public interest that the brakes and clutch of an automobile be in the same relative position on every car we drive," Fisher explained. "Yet under existing law, one who holds the rights to a computer interface may find it in his interest not to share that interface with others on reasonable terms. Not sharing interface designs will be particularly appealing to a rights holder that already has a substantial share of the market."

Recognizing the importance of compatibility and interoperability as a selling feature, most vendors now participate in standards-setting organizations, seeking to foster the agreement on standards that complement their products and their development and marketing strategies. The process of setting standards, however, is a delicate one, as described below. While nurturing compatibility, standards also present the risk of freezing technology at a premature stage. Once in place, standards—even bad ones—are hard to change, perhaps resulting in costs that exceed the benefits of interoperability. Thus, factored into the complex calculus of protections for software must be considerations of how the law accommodates or inhibits interoperability, as well as flexibility in changing standards in tandem with technological advances.

## Open Interfaces, a Controversial Suggestion

Building on the notion that software is unfinished componentry, part of a larger system, Aion's Reinstein advocated that all interfaces be classified as "open." Noting that ideas are often an inseparable part of the interface definition, Reinstein said, "The simplest, most disentangling position I can take is let us just not protect interfaces. Let us invest in the expression of them underneath, and have that be the protected part" of the software product. "Interfaces are legitimate points of competitive entry," and "openness" is a "critical element of software competitiveness," he said.

Copying of interface code, including automated reverse engineering, should not be allowed, he explained. Rather, the implementation should be licensable, and the specification of an interface should be available for others to implement independently. Third parties would avoid the cost of development incurred by the innovator, Reinstein acknowledged, but they would have to invest in writing the code to support the interface.

Those opposed to a flat declaration that all interfaces should be open maintain that the decision of whether to make the specification publicly available is a choice for firms to make. In addition, objectors contend that nearly all elements of a program, including those that connect subroutines and other internal parts of the program, can be construed as interfaces. Consequently, an open-interface rule would render all expressions within a program vulnerable to copying and to misappropriation of the program's functionality. Copyright protection, say those who object to the notion of open interfaces, would become meaningless. It is therefore not surprising that industry views on this issue are very strongly held, because the commercial interests at stake are perceived as vital by many firms.

Addressing these latter concerns, Reinstein defined three categories of "public" interfaces. The first category, and least controversial one, includes interfaces that innovators, perhaps motivated by marketing considerations, have declared to be open. In his second category, Reinstein places interfaces that are "clearly discernible through normal use," a characterization most relevant to user interfaces. This is a determination for the industry to make, he said, but if there is "general agreement" that a user interface, particularly its appearance, fits in this category, then it should be available for others to use or emulate. Finally, interfaces that are "separately priced, separately distributed, or separately packaged" (a language or database management program, for example) are legitimate points of competitive entry, and they should be classified as public, Reinstein said.

Open interfaces, concurred Scott Davis of Digital Equipment Corp., would focus competition on providing "better implementations of standards. That is where the competition can be, and a better implementation may mean something like improved performance, or it might mean security features" that are not offered with other implementations.

Vanguard Atlantic's Lee Keet was among those who faulted the proposal. "I generally agree," he said, "that the utilitarian aspect of the interface should be open for all to use, but I do point out that, in many cases, interfaces have . . . artistic aspects," which warrant protection.

### Immediate Declaration of Rights

The Association of Data Processing Service Organizations (ADAPSO) has been considering a proposed seven-point set of guidelines to clarify whether interfaces and languages are public or proprietary. "Declarations or waivers of proprietary interest in an external interface or language," the proposed guidelines recommend, "should be made specifically and separately, and on a timely basis." Among the problems that would be eliminated with industry-wide adherence to this general rule would be disputes that arise when claims of ownership are delayed and, in the interim, firms presume that use is condoned.

Esther Dyson, while stressing that protection should be accorded only to software elements that meet "high standards of originality," also endorsed immediate declaration of ownership rights. "[T]he job of the vendor is to define his product, to define what he considers to be original, and to sell that. The changes you are seeing in software mean that specification is almost indistinguishable from the implementation. That is why you need [a high standard of] originality, because if anything you specify ends up being protectable, you have a mess. But you can't just protect the implementation . . . [when specification and implementation are] transformable into each other."

Uncertain of the practicality of such an approach, Pamela Samuelson of the University of Pittsburgh explained that firm-initiated declarations of originality and ownership would be inimical to the procedures required for securing a patent. Patent law, she pointed out, requires owners to show that an innovation satisfies the conditions necessary for protection. Particularly for software elements that have features that seem to fall in the gap between copyright and patent law, "I don't think the right solution is . . . just to say it is your property, and then everything will work out," Samuelson said. "In the Anglo-American tradition, the government, through its patent and copyright laws, defines the kinds of innovations that are eligible for protection, the criteria that must be met to qualify for protection, and the extent of protection the law will give to the innovation (both as to duration and as to scope). If you don't follow the procedures, you don't qualify under the criteria, or the thing you want to protect is considered by the law to be unprotectable; in general, the innovation can be freely copied by competitors, whether the innovator likes it or not."

Concerns about the length of protection afforded by patents (17 years) and copyrights (50 years or more) were expressed by several forum participants, who preferred terms that reflected the rapid pace of development in the industry. To assure that important innovations are available for others to build on, a few suggested that mandatory licensing of patented and copyrighted works be required after an initial one- or two-year period of exclusive use. And to spur dissemination of innovations and to encourage firms to offer their best technologies as industry standards, some participants recommended that standards bodies allow the innovators of standards to receive royalties in return for use of their technology. Some of these bodies now make no- or low-cost licensing a condition for adopting a technology as a standard.

## Standardization

By one estimate, more than 1,000 standards pertaining to computer-related technology have either been adopted or are pending before national and international standards-setting bodies (Gantz, 1989). This high level of activity is symptomatic of snowballing consumer demand not only for compatibility of information-related equipment, but also for interoperability of software, allowing independent, perhaps geographically isolated applications to work cooperatively.

Unsatisfied with the computer sector's progress toward these ideals, groups of users are nudging vendors toward standardization—sometimes forcefully. General Motors and other manufacturing concerns organized to develop the manufacturing automation protocol, or MAP, which specifies the standards that vendors of software and information-related equipment must conform to if they wish to sell their products to consortium members and other firms that are following the MAP lead. Another large customer, the U.S. Department of

Defense, continues to forge ahead with its 16-year-old effort to impose a universal computer language—Ada—on its suppliers.

Given the intensity of user wants, companies face a "real risk of being bypassed by the marketplace by being too restrictive in authorizing the use of the expression in [their] protocols," IBM's Figueroa explained.

Yet standardization can be a contentious affair, influenced to some degree by the nature of intellectual property protection. Companies jockey to have their way of doing things accepted, formally or informally, as the industry standard. Losing a standards "battle" means either that a firm will be forced to jettison part or all of its particular approach and to begin anew, or that it can proceed with its proprietary technology, hoping to convince users that the merits of its approach exceed the benefits of compatibility. Moreover, as already mentioned, a firm that has invested heavily in developing a new technology may balk at the prospect of making freely available an innovation that, if made a standard, could make other companies more competitive.

In the international arena, national interests can undermine formal standardization efforts. With each participating country accorded an equal vote, members of international standards-setting bodies may endorse implementations that are perceived to be most beneficial to regional business interests. Compromise is difficult, and if it is reached, the resultant standards may be based on inferior technology. This danger, however, is also present in national standardization efforts.

Users tend to favor standardization because it allows them to choose from among the offerings of different vendors, freeing them from the idiosyncrasies and, thus, incompatibilities of proprietary systems. In turn, compatibility fosters the growth of computer networks that, at the beckoning of the user, can integrate applications unhampered by worries about which vendors made the various software elements needed to solve a specific problem and whether the necessary elements can work together. From the vantage point of individual software products, compatibility greatly increases value because of so-called network externalities—the benefits that accrue to being part of a larger system. Therefore small companies are also likely to be proponents of standardization because their product lines rarely attain the critical mass of offerings necessary to address the majority of user needs. Compatibility affords the opportunity to compete by adding value in areas neglected by dominant firms. Large firms, in contrast, provide a diversity of products that, in effect, already compose a network. Thus the benefits that accrue with compatibility—principally, expanded markets—are likely to be smaller for companies that already have significant shares of the market. "The gains you get from making your market a little bigger," explained Stanley M. Besen, senior economist at the Rand Corporation, "may be relatively small compared to the losses you get by making your market more competitive."

In theory, standardization reduces redundant variety and inefficiency. "We might be better off with fewer things created if they were more widely disseminated," Besen said. "The idea is not to maximize the number of things, but to maximize the value of the things that are created, and that might, in fact, involve fewer things that are more widely disseminated." Without standards, firms may engage in strategies that result in spurious differentiation of products; innovation may be devoted less to adding value and more to creating difference for difference's sake.

Once an industry agrees on a standard, firms can focus their research and development efforts on areas that are said to be "on top" of the standard, where innovation is likely to produce greater functional benefits. In other words, standards are like a foundation upon which innovation can build. "What you want to do," said Scott Davis, senior consulting engineer at the Digital Equipment Corp., "is build on what somebody else has built and not reinvent what was on the bottom."

But variety also has positive attributes that can be erased by standardization. The primary argument against standardization posits that it may freeze technology at a premature stage of development. Standards should not be regarded as the final "best solution, but as temporary rigidity," advised Esther Dyson, publisher of "Release 1.0." "They are like the San Andreas fault. They hold things together for a while, but underneath and around and ahead of the standards, things are changing. You don't want to ratify standards so strongly that they prevent progress. . . . So, standards are not forever. Standards get superseded."

In fact, added Davis, standards are rarely the best solution to a particular need, even when they are new. "Standards tend to be least-common-denominator kinds of solutions," he said, "so that you are not able to take full advantage of the underlying system, the underlying implementation." In the case of de jure standardization, part of the reason why standards fall short of the technological optimum stems from the need for compromise among the many participants in the process. In the case of de facto standardization, the candidate that prevails may be the product of chance occurrences, or the decision may be dictated by the actions of a dominant firm. In either situation, the resultant standard is not necessarily the best of the options available.

## THE INFLUENCE OF INTELLECTUAL PROPERTY LAW

Although easy access to innovations and widespread dissemination of ideas are generally recognized goals of intellectual property law, it does not necessarily follow that compatibility, a means to achieving these goals, is also an aim of the law. Indeed, the courts have been somewhat equivocal in their handling of the issue. In *Apple Computer, Inc. v. Franklin Computer Co.* (545 F. Supp. 812 [E.D. Pa. 1982], Aff'd. 714 F.2d 1240 [3rd Cir. 1983]), in which Franklin was found to have copied Apple's operating system, the Court of Appeals for the Third Circuit found the copyright infringer's compatibility argument less than compelling.

"Franklin," it said, "may wish to achieve total compatibility with independently developed applications programs written for the Apple II, but that is a commercial and competitive objective which does not enter into the somewhat metaphysical issue of whether particular ideas and expression have merged."

In another case, *E.F. Johnson Co. v. Uniden Corp.* (623 F. Supp. 1485 [D. Minn. 1985]), the Federal District Court in Minnesota was more sympathetic to compatibility concerns. At issue was whether the Uniden Corporation copied the software in the E.F. Johnson Company's mobile radio system and, in so doing, infringed Johnson's copyright. Uniden contended that it copied only those elements necessary to achieve compatibility. Duplication of one element of Johnson's software was necessary to achieve compatibility, the court found, but "virtually all other aspects of the defendant's [Uniden's] program could have been independently created, however, without violence to defendant's compatibility objective." The court ruled that Uniden did violate Johnson's copyright, but the decision suggests that copying is permissible when it is the "only and essential means of creating" compatible software.

"The issue of whether the merger-of-ideas-and-expression defense should prevail in cases involving the need for compatibility is an important one," Besen said, "especially for software."

Not everyone agrees, however, that software compatibility is an overriding need, dismissing this claim as a guise for abetting widespread copying of successful products. John Shoch said he regarded as "specious, even pernicious" the argument that an innovator whose product holds sizable market share must surrender his intellectual property to competitors. For a competitor to assert that his program must be compatible with the market leader, who, therefore, "must lose some of his protection . . . ," he said, "is the silliest thing I have ever heard of. The fact that you have been successful does not, by definition, expose you to that loss of your rights."

Promoting compatibility may make business sense, Shoch said, but the decision of whether to pursue this strategy should rest with companies, not with the law.

Intellectual property law, however, does influence the pace at which software compatibility and interoperability evolve in the industry, as well as the nature of the standards that are adopted. "Standards are a strategic tool [that] can be used to [a firm's] advantage or disadvantage," Besen said. The magnitude of either one is determined in large part by the scope of protection for the standardized technology.

With weaker protection, which makes it easier to adopt parts of another's invention, "participants' interests are more closely aligned," access to the standardized technology is not impeded, and competition is more likely to be *within* the standard, Joseph Farrell, a professor of economics at the University of California, Berkeley, has written (Farrell, 1989, p. 16). Strong protection for the standardized technology, in contrast, would force competition into incompatible channels. Such a situation could either foster spurious differentiation of products, or it could push product development into new directions, resulting in socially useful innovations. In his paper, Farrell further elaborates on how intellectual property protection influences standardization, suggesting that copyright may impede the process because of its presumed aversion to function:

> [S]ince copyright protection is broadest where the expression is most arbitrary, useful innovations may go unprotected while arbitrary choices of user interface, for instance, may be held to be protected and may generate large rents if they become de facto market standards.
>
> In the case of traditional creative works, such as novels, protection of an arbitrary creation does not constrain later innovators. If the first innovator's choice of expression is "arbitrary," she could equally well have made any of a number of other choices, and it might seem to follow logically that a later innovator's options are not unduly constrained: he need only avoid consciously doing the same as the first innovator, and this might not seem unduly burdensome. Indeed, in a traditional "decreasing-returns" economy, he will prefer to avoid direct competition with the first innovator, and would have no motive to imitate except for the wish to save costs by slavish copying rather than performing independent work.
>
> But this argument fails to hold in a market characterized by dynamic increasing returns, such as market externalities. Then, the mere fact that a previous innovator used a certain arbitrary expression, and customers have grown used to it, makes that arbitrary expression an important and no longer arbitrary aspect of design. Although, *ex ante*, English could just as well have been written right-to-left as left-to-right, a publisher who tried to introduce that convention now would surely fail.

Left unanswered in this analysis, however, is the recurring question of how to distinguish between useful innovations, ideas, and creative expression. In the copyright area, for example, controversy surrounds the granting of protection for the "look and feel" and the "structure, sequence, and organization" of programs. Critics of the decision in *Whelan v. Jaslow*, for example, argue that the decision awarded protection for an idea, not the expression of the idea. Because of the presumed unavailability of patent protection for software, say others, the court was forced to rely on copyright law to address a matter of software functionality—"structure, sequence, and organization"—that is more appropriately an issue for patent law. Meanwhile, as the number of software-related patents mounts, there are fears that broad ideas, rather than useful innovations or embodiments of ideas, are being granted monopoly-like protection. Making the waters even murkier is the lack of clarity in court rulings on whether firms can adopt elements of competitors' software to achieve compatibility.

## WITHHOLDING OF SOURCE CODE

In his book *The Mythical Man-Month*, Frederick P. Brooks, Jr., a professor of computer science at the University of North Carolina at Chapel Hill and former IBM project manager who directed the development of the operating system for the IBM System/360 line of mainframe computers, extols the virtues of comprehensive, easily understood documentation of computer programs. Such documentation, Brooks writes, tells the program's "story to the human user" (Brooks, 1975, p. 164). Moreover, "the intimate availability of the source program, line by line, to the reader of the documentation makes possible new techniques" (p. 169).

Brooks's essay preceded by nearly a decade his former employer's decision to adopt what was becoming the standard practice of shipping software products without source code. It was a difficult decision, according to IBM's Peter Schneider, and not only because of its perceived negative impact on users. Schneider noted that many of the improvements IBM had made in its software and some commercially successful products were, in effect, developed by the company's field force and its customers. "The opportunity to do that is now precluded," he explained, "because to build those products they had to have access to our source code, and we no longer allow source code out of our laboratories."

These costs notwithstanding, IBM perceived the need for a "safety net—namely, going to object code only and more restrictive contract terms and conditions"—as more compelling, Schneider said. "The reaction to become more secretive because of the uncertainty of the legal system was a prudent business decision."

The fallout from this nearly industry-wide decision has material-ized in several forms. For example, advocates of no or, at most, weak intellectual property protection for software have argued that the withholding of source code vitiates the analogy between literary works and computer programs, the basis for extending copyright protection to software. If software products are not delivered in a human-read-able form, the argument goes, the expression is not revealed to users, and copyright protection is not warranted.

Users most affected by the denial of source code are those who would like to adapt or customize vendor-supplied software to their own peculiar circumstances or to changing organizational needs. In some instances, vendors will acquiesce to those needs and supply the source code, but only after they are convinced of the integrity of clients' security measures and restricted conditions of use are stipulated in a contract. This compromise solution, however, does not work for all customers, including one of the largest, the federal government.

As part of its "data rights" requirement, the federal government generally requires software vendors to relinquish the source code along with the products they sell to the government. Unconvinced that, in using the source code for its own purposes, the government would not jeopardize their trade secrets, many companies have re-frained from doing business with federal agencies, according to Anita Jones of the University of Virginia, who was one of the founders of a small software firm that made such a decision. Other firms have taken a different tack in addressing this concern. They withhold their most advanced technology and sell to the government only hard-ware and software that are not the state of the art and therefore are cause for less concern if inadvertently revealed to competitors.

This practice is not limited to small business, Jones asserted. "Some very large companies that sell both hardware and software," she said, "have separate divisions to do business with the government . . . . [These firms] do not give those divisions access to their best technology . . . . They phase their commercial divisions into the government divisions as the technology and the manufacturing plants age. I sub-mit to you that that is not in the public's interest and a major reason for that is the government's stance on data rights."

Universities are also hampered by the withholding of source code, Jones maintained, contending that distributing object code only "inhibits the flow of ideas in the university research community. Without source code, and barring reverse engineering of programs," she said, researchers cannot "get the maximum benefit out of new ideas that are in the form of software. That is the only form that is maximally useful."

Through contractual arrangements, some companies will supply source code to scientists, allowing them to make alterations and to experiment with new applications. But contract-imposed restrictions often prevent researchers from sharing this altered code and the resultant innovations with their peers, Jones said. As a consequence of these actions, the industry is handicapping the ability of universities to contribute to software research and development, she claimed. "The universities have fed the high-technology software business to a very large and rich extent, and I don't like to see any constraints on that," Jones said.

The introduction of trade secret law into the academic environment in connection with software and other new technologies can have serious consequences for the traditional academic mission, Reichman maintains. "University professors are habitually slow to consider that they may have illicitly borrowed software solutions covered by proprietary rights," he said. "Copyright law can magnify the ensuing difficulties because it is a field in which innovation occurs through sequential and cumulative improvements, and every researcher making use of another researcher's prior art can expose himself to potential liability for infringement or at least to litigation, absent explicit authorization for use."

Others at the forum questioned whether rigid restrictions on the distribution of source code were inimical to copyright law's fair use doctrine, which permits copying and, perhaps, reverse compilation for research and other noncommercial purposes. Contractual stipulations, however, might block the rights normally afforded by the fair use exception.

## REVERSE ENGINEERING

Copyright's allowance for independent development provides a safe haven for follower firms. For some firms, this safe haven takes the form of a "clean room,"[3] a means of avoiding charges of infringement or at least improving the chances of prevailing against such charges. A firm that desires to copy the idea but not the expression of a competitor's program can isolate its programmers, providing these workers only with a description of the software application they are to emulate. Outside the clean room, other workers may study the manual and other documentation provided with legally obtained software, and they may observe and test the original program while it is running on a computer. These benchmark test results and observations are used to assess the performance and functionality of code written in the clean room. Code that does not achieve the desired level of functionality may be returned to the clean room, perhaps with a more detailed description of the problem, for modification.

This description applies to the purest form of the clean room concept, and it is the software industry counterpart to reverse engineering in industries that manufacture machinery, including computers. In hardware industries, reverse engineering is a common practice, but makers of machinery must not only figure out how the targeted product works, but they must also determine how to manufacture it and develop the necessary assembly process, all of which can take substantial amounts of time and money. Similar investments in manufacturing and technology are not required to reproduce software products. The "purity" of the software clean room is determined by the level of detail in the information that is passed into the room: the more detailed the information—"chunks" of code from the target program, for example—the more suspect the process may become and the more likely the clean room program will be similar to the original.

The great temptation in developing software, of course, is to use reverse compilation technology, which, as IBM's Figueroa explained, "facilitates the low-cost adaptation of the protected expression in the original program, resulting in the quick and cheap generation of a competing program. Thus, the program creator has his lead time erased, his price undercut, and his market reduced for the very thing he created."

According to Schneider, also of IBM, reverse compilation and subsequent changes in code, data structure, or other components can yield a program that, although the product of illegal copying, bears little, if any, provable resemblance to the original. If the designers and programmers of the original work find it difficult to determine whether a program is a copy, as Schneider maintained is often the case, then judges, who are not schooled in the technology, may have an especially hard time assessing whether a program is a derivative work and, therefore, infringes on the original.

## CONCLUSION

Ideally, explained Francis Fisher, incentives, or the monopoly rights that serve as the "carrot" to induce innovation, will yield "access to goods and services, including ideas and expressions, for a price that is as close to cost as possible. . . . Monopoly profits beyond those needed to cover costs are not in the public interest." Thus an effective intellectual property system should contribute to efficiently operating national and international markets, and at the same time fairly reward investment, creative genius, and hard work and drive firms to pursue successive rounds of innovation. But it cannot do so unless the costs associated with unsuccessful risks are included. It is the risk in creation, not the cost of production, that intellectual property protection must reward.

Yet in the real world, optima are rarely achieved, forcing a pragmatic consideration that recognizes that a productive balance between protection and dissemination is a shifting target. "What bad behavior will be tolerated," asked Bricklin, "so as not to throw out the baby with the bath water?" Measures crafted to address one wrong, such as automatic cloning of programs, could have the unintended, negative consequences of inhibiting independent innovation—a common occurrence, according to Bricklin, in software development—or of discouraging other desirable aspects of the behavior of innovators and investors.

Even if the existing framework of intellectual property law is eventually deemed satisfactory, clarification of the scope and applicability of both patent and copyright law was described by forum participants as a critical need. "What we are looking for," said John Shoch, "is a consistent and unified way to deal with the issues of software and intellectual property." Because such a holistic perspective, one that provides a comprehensible set of guidelines for investors and software developers, does not now exist, more litigation is a prospect for the software industry. According to several legal experts at the forum, that is an almost absolute certainty. But the likelihood of more legal disputes should not be surprising, given the inevitable lag between the rate of technological advance and the slower pace at which the law responds.

## NOTES

1. Results of the survey were reported in "Release 1.0," August 21, 1989, 89-8, p. 3.

2. Paraphrase of comments made by Gordon Moore, chairman, Intel Corp., at the May 1989 CSTB Colloquium on Competitiveness.

3. In this usage, *clean room* is a metaphor for a software development workplace uncontaminated by familiarity with the expression of a competitor's product. In the manufacture of semiconductors, great expense is taken to isolate workers from contamination by minuscule amounts of dust. Hence the metaphor.

If you limit protection, you are going to end up in a world of stagnation and trade secrets.

—Esther Dyson, *Publisher, "Release 1.0"*

The bottom line is that we decided to invest in software development as a separate business, and we based our decision to put significant resources into that business on the expectation that we could protect the expression in our programs from copying.

—Howard G. Figueroa, *Vice President, Commercial and Industry Relations, IBM Corp.*

Saying it is okay to do nothing because things will work out strikes me as analogous to the response given by the man who jumped off the top of the Empire State Building. When asked as he passed the 50th floor, "How's it going?", he replied, "So far, terrific." So cautious, thoroughgoing inquiry seems to me to be really justified here.

—Mitchell D. Kapor, *Chairman, ON Technology, Inc.*

I am appalled by the crudity of the discussion right now in the industry around what is interface and what is functionality. I think that we should do a whole lot more worrying about the way these expressions and the way this creativity break out in pieces and in components.

—Frank Ingari, *Vice President, Spreadsheet Division, Lotus Development Corp.*

There has to be some way of recognizing the economic value and importance of existing standards, conventions, and user interface models, and yet be able to build on it at a reasonable cost.

—Robert Spinrad, *Director, Corporate Technology, Xerox Corp.*

# 5

# The Open Agenda

The aim of this project was to advance the state of knowledge and the quality of the public policy debate on intellectual property protection issues for software by bringing together an array of interested parties. This area of technology remains in rapid transition, and there are not simple solutions to the complex problems it presents. While a broad analytic structure remains a future goal and a worthy objective of public policy research, the two-day forum whose discussions are summarized here was an important step in aiding the communications among the technical and legal experts who often use different vocabularies and have conflicting problem-solving approaches.[1]

Software is evolving from a technology originally conceived as a flexible and inexpensive mechanism for controlling computer hardware to products that embody the functional processes and knowledge base of entire industries and dominate the costs of computer usage. Thus the intrinsic value of software, apart from its form of expression, is hard to quantify, but it is rapidly growing and constitutes the asset end users as well as software vendors seek to protect.

A snapshot of the current technology shows evidence of the evolution of the field, with different strands overlapping. That picture reveals that part of the enterprise resembles the highly experimental and entrepreneurial situation of 25 years ago, complete with computer hackers, developers producing "freeware," and highly innovative individuals working in isolation. At the same time, however, it also reflects a major industry dedicated to building reliable, well-maintained software for the efficient execution of well-established applications. Software users cover an equally broad range, from millions of novice users to giant corporations whose software expertise rivals (and sometimes exceeds) that of their software suppliers.

With as much diversity and heterogeneity as are found in this sector, it should not be a surprise that discussions involving intellectual property protection for software should generate great controversy and complicate agreement on a national policy agenda. The questions involved in the debate—what to protect, how to protect it, and for how long—call for value judgments in a large community with few shared values.

Because software is so malleable, representing information in many forms (images, sounds, data, and words) and providing the means for creating as well as transmuting and transmitting it, there was little agreement except in general terms on how to describe the values embodied in software. Thus there is less agreement on what aspects of software should, in the public interest, be protected as personal or business property. Complicating the discussion further is the absence of unambiguous technical or legal definitions of some of the key terms of the discussion, for example, a software *interface*. Not only did the technical and legal experts use the word very differently on occasion, but even the experts also used the term slightly differently, depending on their professional perspective or segment of the industry.

Software is of great economic and functional value to society. It is important that software protection not be thought of as an end in itself, but rather as a part of the incentive structure leading to the creation, diffusion, and use of software innovations. Differences of opinion over software protection should not be seen as a battle between opposing economic interests—a struggle among vendors and between them and their customers. Rather, the pressing issues revolve around the incentives—and disincentives—that are provided for creativity, for entrepreneurial risk, for quality services to end users, and for a stable, competitive marketplace.

Few would deny that the pace of software innovation and the growth of the industry attest to the strength of the incentives and the adequacy of safeguards to date. The question is whether technological and legal developments in the future will combine to enhance or undermine those incentives and safeguards. At the root of the debate about software protection is not the preservation of the property rights of its creators, but the extent to which protection of those rights will promote innovation without retarding technical progress or inducing in the market an instability that might deprive software users of good service as well as new capabilities.

Just as technological change affects the evolution of legal principles, so also will legal rulings affect the manner in which technical progress unfolds. For technological reasons, progress in computer hardware has been even more rapid than that in software for many years. Thus, in spite of extraordinary industry growth, software costs and complexity have become the pacing factor in the implementation of many worthwhile applications. At issue now is whether legal developments will widen or narrow the software bottleneck to progress.

While recognizing that questions arise at the margins of copyright and patent law, several legal experts advised that the current level of uncertainty should not be interpreted as proof of the inadequacy of either body of law. "One of the factors that is operating here," Goldberg suggested, "is perhaps a philosophic discomfort with things or concepts that can't be easily pigeon-holed . . . in the fashion of binary digits—being either-or." He continued, "It is the nature of the legal process that it develops. It cannot be handed down from Capitol Hill with pristine purity and crystalline clarity in its application to all circumstances for all time."

Indeed, most should not be and some cannot be. Automated reverse-engineering and recompilation techniques, for example, may be used to create derivative products that offer the same functionality as the original software but are so dissimilar in appearance and structure that even the most astute judges and juries will be hard-pressed to identify illegal copying. The answer to that problem may be technological, such as "fingerprinting" or otherwise identifying the source of derivative works. Or it may be the fact that products created this way may be more costly to maintain and evolve than is original software created from scratch. Yet other important questions fall squarely within the realm of the law, or into the gray area between accepted business practices and law. Different views exist on how best to proceed.

## DEFINING A CONCEPT OF VALUE

Lotus's Frank Ingari struck a responsive chord when he asserted the need to define for software a concept of value that can serve as a lens for evaluating intellectual property issues. Too little discussion, he maintained, is devoted to determining what to protect and why.

"We are sort of at the second-order discussion already," he explained. "Is copyright better? What is good for the industry? What is good for the Third World? Everybody is taking positions on what is good for whom, and I don't see much discussion of what we are trying to protect in the first place."

Esther Dyson, publisher of "Release 1.0," concurred. "The real issue here is defining intellectual property," she said. "We can work out what the law does if we can define the stuff that we are trying to protect." Dyson advised, however, that the value of different software components will change as the technology advances, making value an evolving concept.

Initially, she said, "virtually the only thing you wanted to protect in software was the code. Then we got into the 'look and feel issue.' As we move on toward object-oriented code, we are going to have these modules of functionality that are specifically designed to be reused. But the people who design them are still going to want to protect them, charge for them, and so we are going to have a much more complicated problem in the future, . . . when bits of software have to work together."

Before deferring intellectual property matters to lawyers, it was suggested, software firms may be better served by first determining what elements of software are most beneficial to users, the ultimate judges of value. "I am appalled by the crudity of the discussion right now in the industry around what is interface and what is functionality," Ingari said. "I think we should do a whole lot more worrying about the way these expressions and this creativity break out in pieces and components."

Establishing a common understanding of software, as both a functional, marketable good and as the product of a complex design and engineering process, serves two necessary purposes. First, it provides perspective on where the value, or intellectual property, lies in a particular piece of software and, therefore, on what elements warrant protection. Second, a broadly accepted notion of software—one that embraces its numerous manifestations and its complex underpinnings—can guide the application of intellectual property law.

## LEGISLATIVE "SOLUTIONS"?

Few would quibble with the goals for the intellectual property system Robert Spinrad suggests (Box 5.1), but most would argue about measures proposed to achieve them, which range, as Mitchell Kapor pointed out, from "doing nothing" to "doing something radical."

Most radical of all perhaps are proposals to create a sui generis system, a body of law specific to software. An argument advanced in support of this notion contends that, at least in the copyright area, attempts to address issues related to the functionality of software are distorting the law. As a result, the argument continues, a sui generis system for software is evolving piecemeal through the case law—

---

### BOX 5.1—SUGGESTED GOALS FOR THE INTELLECTUAL PROPERTY SYSTEM

While leaving legal specifics for others to debate, Robert Spinrad of Xerox Corp. offered a set of general goals for the intellectual property system to achieve. Comments by forum participants suggested that Spinrad's desiderata encapsulated the essential requirements of innovators and investors. His criteria—"The Five Cs"—are summarized below.

Coverage, or protection, should extend to the "brilliant idea" embodied in a software product. "This is certainly something you want to be able to protect and own and control the future of," Spinrad said. Protection should also be accorded the programming efforts, the "hard work" that transforms the idea into a marketable product.

Continuity, "the ability to build on existing standards and conventions at reasonable cost," is necessary to create a foundation upon which the software industry can build. "Access, not appropriation [is key]," Spinrad said, acknowledging that "reasonable cost" is not easily defined. Yet, he added, arbitrary rules or constraints should not "force the programs that work on [the user's] behalf to use different interfaces, to meet different standards, . . . to follow different protocols. So, there has to be some way of being able to build one brick on top of another."

Consistency in the application and scope of intellectual property protections affords the "predictability, the calculability" that firms require to make the marketing and development decisions that dictate the allocation of financial resources and personnel. Surprises, such as those that might result as belated declarations of property rights, compound the unavoidable uncertainties of the marketplace.

Cognizance, "the timely awareness of other intellectual property rights claims," minimizes the danger of being blindsided by competitors. "I don't want to be put in a position of developing a product," Spinrad explained, "only to discover a year after it is on the market—or, even more frightening, just as it is about to hit the market—that an essential element of it is something that had been percolating through the patent process and that, because of the confidentiality [of the process], I didn't know it was coming."

Convenience, or a straightforward intellectual property system that minimizes the need for litigation, may be the equivalent of "asking for the moon," Spinrad said. Nonetheless, he added, "I would like a minimum amount of conflict about which set of rules or . . . statutes cover" which aspects of software.

---

without the benefit of the foresight that would go into a deliberately crafted set of laws.

Mention the term *sui generis* at a gathering devoted to software-related legal issues, however, and strenuous objections are sure to follow. One frequent criticism holds that abandoning a long-standing body of laws—albeit laws that did not anticipate the development of software—for an entirely new system would increase uncertainty, not reduce it.

"I think what we might be faced with," said Ron Palenski, counsel for the Association of Data Processing Service Organizations (ADAPSO), "is a conflict between a slower societal process to resolve these issues in a more rapidly moving marketplace and more rapidly moving technology. I would submit, even if you went to a different system, you would still find the same problems."

Added attorney Ronald Laurie of Irell & Manella, "I buy copyright, as opposed to intermediate solutions, because the law in this country, whether we like it or not, evolves interstitially in court. And as someone who spends a lot of time in court, I would feel much more comfortable arguing my case by analogy." Moreover, laws drafted to address today's concerns could be rendered obsolete by future advances in technology, which will engender unanticipated legal issues.

That most litigators present at the forum prefer evolutionary development of case law, within the framework of current copyright and patent statutes, reflects more than confidence that the law is sufficiently elastic to fit evolving circumstances. Their preference may also indicate a lower confidence in the legislative process as the alternative. These litigators share with the scientists an awareness of rapid technological change in the industry but tend to opt for a more surprise-free venue for legal change, while the scientists more willingly contemplate the sui generis approach.

The chorus of objections that greets proposals for new legal approaches shifts attention to the other pole in the range characterized by Kapor—the "do nothing" option. Howard Figueroa espoused this view, noting that many of the issues and concerns now being debated were addressed more than 20 years ago, when firms first contemplated "unbundling" software from their hardware products.[2]

"The bottom line is that we decided to invest in software development as a separate business," Figueroa explained, "and we based our decision to put significant resources into that business on the expectation that we could protect the expression in our programs from copying. "Copyright protection would apply to that product expression per se. It would require no up-front expenditure to obtain that protection, and it was and is international in scope. We felt that we could build a separate business on this type of protection."

Figueroa maintained that the existing intellectual property system works, and he recommended a hands-off approach toward copyright law. "I fundamentally believe," he said, "that there is no reason to make any specific changes in relationship to the copyright law as it is currently constituted. . . . I think that what we should be relying upon is the evolution of the law as it is interpreted in the courts. . . ."

While many in the software industry favor staying within the existing legal structure, a substantial number believe that the system should provide better guidance and that copyright and patent laws could be applied more coherently. Thus it is the vast middle ground between the extremes of a do-nothing approach and a sui generis system where most of the discussion and most of the disagreement occur.

Kapor was among several technical experts who stressed the need at least to reassess the appropriateness of maintaining the status quo. "[S]aying it is okay to do nothing because things will work out," he said, "strikes me as analogous to the response given by the man who jumped off the top of the Empire State Building. When asked as he passed the 50th floor, 'How's it going?', he replied, 'So far, terrific.' So cautious, thoroughgoing inquiry seems to me to be really justified here."

## HYBRID SYSTEM FOR HYBRID TECHNOLOGIES?

Perhaps neither set of principles is appropriate for software—at least not in their current form. This view is espoused by Vanderbilt University law professor Jerome Reichman, who distinguishes between the mature copyright paradigm of artistic property law and a modified copyright approach better suited to what he calls "intermediate technologies" falling below the patent and copyright paradigms (Reichman, 1989). His review of international intellectual property laws leads him to conclude that software is the most recent manifestation of "hybrid technologies" that reside in the murky region between patentable inventions and copyrightable creative works. The intellectual property system, he said, carves the universe of created works into art, the province of copyright law, and inventions, the province of patent law. But software, like industrial designs and architectural and engineering drawings, embodies properties of both categories and, therefore, distorts the tenets of patent and copyright law. Historically, nations have differed in their legal treatment of these hybrid technologies, placing them in one category or the other and sometimes oscillating between categories. The results, Reichman said, have never been satisfactory, generating a "cycle of overprotection and underprotection."

Problems have been most acute for industrial designs and works of applied art, which are governed concurrently by the copyright and the industrial property treaties. According to Reichman, both industrial art (i.e., designs) and industrial literature (i.e., software) "bear technological and applied scientific know-how on their face." The ingenuity and skilled effort that go into making software and other design-intensive works cannot be hidden, he said. Rather, they are transferred along with the product.

Recognizing this vulnerability to easy duplication, many nations have chosen to protect these works through copyright law because, for one reason, it does not discriminate on the basis of merit. According to Reichman, copyright law accepts all comers and it allows the market to determine value, the very opposite of patent law, which requires the patent examiner to determine merit according to the novelty and nonobviousness standards. From a behavioral standpoint, investors in applied scientific know-how find copyright attractive because of its inherent disposition to supply artificial lead time to all comers without regard to innovative merit (Reichman, 1991). While the protection afforded by the full copyright paradigm attracts investors in applied scientific know-how, Reichman finds that this paradigm becomes counterproductive over time because its wide protective net soon frustrates the very incremental innovation that sought copyright protection in the first instance.

Efforts to protect design-intensive works under patent law are undermined by that law's standards of nonobviousness and novelty. Although the works are largely utilitarian and sold in markets for nonartistic and nonliterary products (properties that align them with patented inventions), they usually embody incremental improvements on known solutions, Reichman said. Incremental innovation is legally obvious by definition and therefore is unprotectable. To grant patents for works that do not attain the high level of originality required for other technologies is to disrupt the patent system, he said.

Thus Reichman proposes that a modified copyright approach is more appropriate for applied scientific expertise, including software, and other hybrid technologies than either the mature copyright or patent models that underlie the world's intellectual property system as it stands. He underscores the need to reckon with what he believes is a potentially serious problem, the danger of unreasonably long periods of protection for useful works and the consequent danger of disrupting market competition. Under copyright law, owners of software innovations, which have an essentially machine-like utility, would hold exclusive rights for up to 100 years. "No industrial property, no innovation—whether a computer program or a cancer cure or a gene splice—should conceivably be protected for 75 to 100 years on the products market," Reichman said.

Although protection for the better part of a century does seem excessive for any utilitarian product, the discomfort may derive more from appearances than actual harm. Given the rate of progress in computer technology, it is hard to imagine any piece of utilitarian software having market value after 10 or 20 years at most. In any case if only the expression is protected, and not the function, the independent implementation of that function in new software need not be seriously impeded by an overlong period of copyright protection. And all users of the software can experience and learn from the functional utility of a program. An approach to correcting the deficiencies that Reichman perceives in the legal treatment of software and other design-intensive works is to create a third category of intellectual property for hybrid technologies.

Echoing Reichman's reasoning, L. Thorne McCarty, a professor of computer science and law at Rutgers University, suggested that software may represent a new type of intellectual effort. The skilled effort that software development requires, he said, "does not rise to patent-level protection, not on obvious things." Yet, McCarty added, copyright in its current form might not offer sufficient protection against reverse engineering methods that make it increasingly difficult to distinguish between copying and independent innovation.

## INCREMENTAL IMPROVEMENTS TO PATENT SYSTEM?

Defenders of the current system counter that it is far better to adapt known approaches evolutionarily than to create a new category of protection with all the attendant uncertainties that would ensue. Although there is sharp disagreement over the appropriateness of patent protection for software, even its most ardent advocates find the current patent system to be deficient in some structural and administrative areas. Donald Chisum of the University of Washington, a strong proponent of patents for software, listed problems in the procurement and enforcement of patents, none of them peculiar to software. While Chisum sees these problems as affecting all technologies, others view the consequences as more severe for software.

The need to improve and speed the Patent and Trademark Office's handling of applications is often cited as one such concern. Chisum noted that virtually all other countries publish claims within 18 months of the filing date. In the United States, the patent approval process takes nearly twice as long, greatly increasing the chance that an innovator will be blindsided by a competitor whose application was filed earlier. The danger is substantially increased by the prevailing practice of shipping software products in object code. A notification of "patents pending" is of little assistance to a competitor who is unable to reverse compile the product and understand it.

Participants also complained of the difficulty of tracking existing software patents, a problem that also increases the risk of unintentional infringement. The dangers of pursuing an innovation that may already be patented or that may be in the patent-review pipeline are of grave concern to developers. According to Dyson, publisher of "Release 1.0," the first concern could be assuaged by a "meaningful, automatically updating electronic database that contains information on patented technologies."

Currently, searches of patent literature are error-prone exercises, incurring a high risk of overlooking relevant subject matter because of the fragmented, disorganized state of patent information. To correct this shortcoming, Esther Dyson proposed that the Patent and Trademark Office create a database that describes existing software, which would help innovators determine the "prior art" in the field.[3] The second issue, that of losing out to a competitor whose application was submitted earlier, is more problematic because of the short life cycle of software products. Thus the competitor who loses out on a patent has the option of licensing the innovation from the patent holder, if that option exists, or of foregoing the next generation of the product-development cycle. Eventually, warns Brian Kahin, the rapid rate of innovation in the software industry will be slowed to conform with the pace of the patent review and approval process.

Finally, several participants advocated establishment of an industrial advisory board to help Patent and Trademark Office personnel improve their expertise in the software area. Those who question the appropriateness of patents for software-related inventions include these shortcomings in their appraisals, but only as a starting point that leads to more fundamental concerns.

Even the most ardent advocates of software patents acknowledge that patents issued for broad ideas pose potential problems for the industry. Kapor, who counted himself as neither proponent nor opponent, believes this to be an especially serious problem, the impact of which has yet to be felt. A single patent decision that affirms protection for a broad idea, Kapor said, "could change the industry mood from sanguinity to terror."

## NEXT STEPS

The forum discussion reflected a high degree of discomfort by many computer scientists with the intellectual basis for the protection system as it exists. There was considerable uncertainty about how well the system will cope with a wide variety of emerging issues. Many features of the present system—such as the duration of protection for utilitarian software—are recognized as anachronistic. But few would argue that a demand for royalties for use of a 1970-vintage word processor would generate any revenue in 2045. Others were critical of the incremental, somewhat stochastic evolution of legal principles based on case law, but no one presented an attractive proposal for near-term legislative action. Nor did anyone advance evidence that the system the United States has lived with for 30 years has thwarted innovation or failed to produce a business environment that supports rapid growth. Thus considerable common ground united the participants.

Nevertheless, there is much work to be done by technically qualified experts who understand the underlying legal principles and policy issues. Legal scholars will have to continue to pursue the questions that fall within their domain. But the Computer Science and Telecommunications Board, although not competent in the law, has access to a broad range of technical experts, many of whom have been deeply engaged in the legal and political dimensions of their trade. These suggestions for further exploration are addressed to the board.

When the steering committee began preparing for the forum project early in 1989, it was struck by the paucity of scholarly literature on the nature of software, the values it may embody, and the balance of creativity, discipline, structure, and knowledge of applications that underpin those values and lead to excellent products. Copyright protection has operated in the software market during many years when most system software was unique to the hardware it ran on and when there were dozens of word processors, accounting programs, spreadsheets, and device controllers of more or less equivalent merit. Copyright is hospitable to genius and mediocrity alike. End users, not patent examiners, judge the social merit of copyrighted software. Bad programs enjoy the same protection as excellent ones, but so long as it is only their expression that is protected, they are discarded without harm to the industry. The market, not the privilege of limited monopoly, has driven the industry's growth.

But the magnitude of the assets required to launch a successful software project is growing very rapidly, and the constraints on substitution of independent implementations of needed function are rising, too. Barriers to product substitution are rising as industry standards aimed at increased interoperability gain acceptance and end users insist on familiar interfaces. The qualities that are associated with successful products will depend increasingly on collections of talent of a quite unique kind. The incentive to imitate, if not copy, the work of successful software providers will grow. Whether the attributes of patentable invention have their equivalents in software is a matter for debate. But the clamor for incentives to nurture that talent is sure to rise. How then is the rationale for awards of limited monopoly aimed at "advancing the useful arts and sciences" of software to be developed in the absence of a deeper understanding of those unique talents and qualities?

A second, more practical task for computer scientists and lawyers in collaboration is to develop operationally useful characterizations of software attributes that require legal interpretation. Examples might include system-level and user interfaces; languages; the concepts of compilation, decompilation, and restructuring; the distinction between architecture, design, and implementation; and the distinctions between mathematical principles, algorithms, and procedures. These characterizations need to be designed to be adaptable, if not invariant, in the presence of rapid technological change. The value of this effort lies in increased clarity of communication and debate, in court and beyond.

A third area needing study is the implications of a rapid increase in the rate of issuance of patents covering functions embodied in software. Because the increase in rate of filings and the courts' seemingly growing receptivity to the legitimacy of software patents are relatively recent events, it is not possible to point to past growth of the software industry as proof that this growth will not be inhibited or the market disrupted in the future. There are both abstract and practical problems to be addressed. When are clever mathematical procedures intrinsic properties of nature, like Newton's laws of physics, and thus unpatentable? On the practical side, how is either the patent examiner or the software entrepreneur to determine whether a potentially patentable software idea has already been used in available computer code, and is thus part of the prior art? How is the developer of a commercial software offering to be able to ensure that the company's programmers are not reinventing ideas that have been submitted for patents not yet issued? What, indeed, are to be the criteria for "nonobviousness" in software?

What is at stake? The future success of American innovators in an industry with clear global leadership will hinge in large measure on developments in software design houses and the marketplace. The courts and the Congress, however, will delimit the playing field on which software developers compete. They will do this through the rules that they do or do not make or alter. Given the American propensity to litigiousness, and the drag on productivity that many industries have experienced as a result, the software industry is vulnerable. The delicacy of the current balance of protection arrangements for computer software requires respect, even as the issues are vigorously examined. The open and constructive discussion at the forum and the preparatory workshop have made a useful contribution toward a broader understanding of that balance and its implications.

## NOTES

1. The forum started a dialogue that should be continued. The Computer Science and Telecommunications Board is exploring options to further address the issue.

2. The "unbundling" of software and service from hardware sales by IBM was undoubtedly a wise business decision that depended for its success on IBM's copyright in the system software. As described by Howard Figueroa, Thomas Watson, Jr., ascribes the decision in June 1969 to general counsel Burke Marshall's warnings about antitrust exposure. See Watson and Petre (1990).

3. The LEXPAT database can provide easy and rapid access to copies of software patents, if the searcher wishes to examine a particular patent and knows its patent number. Dyson's suggestion differs in that it is proposing a content/area search capability that does not currently exist. Developing the proposed capability would be a major undertaking.

# 6

# Bibliography

Branscomb, Anne W. 1988. "Who owns creativity?" *Technology Review*, May/June, p. 43.

Branscomb, A.W. 1989. Protecting the crown jewels of the information economy—The legal protection of computer software as an intellectual asset: An overview of policy issues for congressional oversight. Statement given before the Subcommittee on Courts, Intellectual Property, and Administration of Justice, U.S. House of Representatives, Washington, D.C., November 8.

Brooks, Frederick P., Jr. 1975. *The Mythical Man-Month*, Addison-Wesley, Reading, Mass.

*Chronicle of Higher Education*. 1989a. "'Electrocopies' seen surpassing photocopies as threat to copyright," March 1.

*Chronicle of Higher Education*. 1989b. "Court will not hear case accusing UCLA of copying software," March 29.

Clapes, Anthony Lawrence. 1989. *Software, Copyright, & Competition: The "Look and Feel" of the Law*, Quorum, New York, p. 143.

Cleveland, H. 1989. "Can intellectual property be protected?" *Change*, May/June, pp. 10-11.

Computer and Business Equipment Manufacturers Association (CBEMA). 1990. *The Information Technology Industry Data Book 1960-2000*, CBEMA, Washington, D.C.

*Computer Week*. 1989. "Criticism builds over impact of look-and-feel litigation," May 1.

*Computerworld*. 1989. "Copyright regulations revised," April.

COPP Report. 1989. *Intellectual Property Protection—a COPP Historical Resume*, IEEE, New York.

Davidson, Duncan M. 1986. "Common law, uncommon software," *University of Pittsburgh Law Review*, Vol. 47, pp. 1037-1117.

Dyson, E. 1989. "Three weeks that shook my world," *Forbes*, June 12, pp. 103-108.

Farrell, Joseph. 1989. "Standardization and intellectual property." Reprint of a talk given at the CESLaST conference, Phoenix, Ariz., February 1989 p. 16.

*Federal Computer Week*. 1989. "Microsoft Corp. downplays Apple display lawsuit," April 10.

Fisher, F.D. 1989. "The electronic lumberyard and builders' rights: technology, copyrights, patents, and academe," *Change*, May/June, pp. 13-21.

Foley, James D. 1987. "Interfaces for advanced computing," *Scientific American*, October, pp. 127-135.

Gantz, John. 1989. "Standards: What they are. What they aren't," *Networking Magazine*, May, p. 23.

Garfinkel, Simson L. 1991. "Programs to the people," *Technology Review* 94(2), February-March, pp. 52-60.

Gasper, Elon, Ed Harris, Paul Heckel, William Hulbig, Larry Lightman, and Mike O'Malley. 1989. "Vital to small companies," *New York Times*, June 8.

Gilbert, S.W. and P. Lyman. 1989. "Intellectual property in the information age: issues beyond the copyright law," *Change*, May/June, pp. 23-28.

Goldberg, Morton and John F. Burleigh. 1989. "Copyright protection for computer programs: Is the sky falling?" America Intellectual Property Law Association, Computer Law Association, New York.

Jorde, T.M. and D.J. Teece. 1989. "Competition and cooperation: Striking the right balance," *California Management Review Reprint Series* 31(3):25-37.

Kahin, Brian. 1989. "Software patents: franchising the information structure," *Change*, May/June, pp. 24-25.

Keefe, Patricia. 1991. "Paperback pulls spreadsheet, won't appeal Lotus victory," *Computerworld*, Oct. 22, p. 7.

Miller, Michael W. 1989. "A brave new world: Streams of 1s and 0s," *Wall Street Journal*, Centennial Edition, p. A-15.

Newell, Allen. 1986. "Response: The models are broken, the models are broken," *University of Pittsburgh Law Review*, Vol. 47, pp. 1023-1035.

Pollack, Andrew. 1990. "Most of Xerox's suit against Apple barred," *New York Times*, March 24, pp. 31 and 33.

Reichman, J.H. 1989. "Computer programs as applied to scientific know-how: Implications of copyright protection for commercialized university research," *Vanderbilt Law Review* 42(3):639-723.

Reichman, J.H. 1991. "Design protection and the new technologies: The United States experience in a transnational perspective," 19 *University of Baltimore Law Review*, Part III, B-3, "Logic of a Modified Copyright Approach" (forthcoming).

Samuelson, P. 1985. "Creating a new kind of intellectual property: Applying the lessons of the chip law to computer programs," *Minnesota Law Review* 70(2):471-531.

Samuelson, P. 1989a. "Why the look and feel of software user interfaces should not be protected by copyright law," *Communications of the ACM* 32(5):563-72.

Samuelson, P. 1989b. "Report on AIPLA survey on the patent/copyright interface for computer programs," May 12, draft.

Samuelson, Pamela. 1988. "Reflections on the state of American software copyright law and the perils of teaching it," *Columbia-VLA Journal of Law & the Arts*, Vol. 13, p. 61.

Scherer, F.M. 1984. *Innovation and Growth*, MIT Press, Cambridge, Mass.

Teece, D.J. 1989. "Inter-organizational requirements of the innovation process," *Managerial and Decision Economics*, Special Issue (John Wiley & Sons, New York), pp. 35-42.

U.S. Department of Commerce. 1991. "Computer equipment and software," *1990 U.S. Industrial Outlook*, pp. 26-31.

U.S. Patent and Trademark Office. 1989. "Patentable subject matter: Mathematical algorithms and computer programs," *Official Gazette*, 1106 OG, September 5.

Verity, John W. 1990. "Defense against pirates or death to the clones?" *Business Week*, May 7.

*Wall Street Journal*. 1989. "Software company wins case alleging violated copyright," March 6.

*Wall Street Journal*. 1989. "U.S. companies curb pirating of some items but by no means all," March 16.

*Wall Street Journal*. 1989. "Apple wins first round in software copyright case," March 22.

*Wall Street Journal*. 1989. "Microsoft sees gain in ruling on Apple's suit," March 22.

*Wall Street Journal*. 1989. "Trade-secret fight imperils a start-up," March 22.

*Wall Street Journal*. 1989. "Three computer industry leaders gird for battle over copyright infringement," April 7.

*Washington Post*. 1989. "From software to sportswear, Bangkok is the capital of counterfeit products," March 12.

*Washington Post*. 1989. "Thailand's refusal to protect copyrights produces cheap goods, disputes with U.S.," March 12.

*Washington Post*. 1989. "The battle over software protection," April 2.

*Washington Post*. 1989. "U.S. businesses urge trade sanctions to stop piracy of software in China," April 10.

Watson, Thomas J., Jr., and Peter Petre. 1990. *Father, Son & Co.*, Bantam Books, New York.

# Appendixes

# Appendix A
# Intellectual Property Challenges in Software
# Workshop Program and Participants*

## PROGRAM

*Tuesday, September 12*

1. **Opening Remarks and Introductions**
   Lewis Branscomb                                    9:00 a.m.

2. **The Environment for Software Five Years**
   **Down the Road**                                  9:15 a.m.

   Paul Goldstein, Organizer & Moderator

   Questions:
   What elements of software are protected by copy-
      right, patents, and trade secrets?
   What protections and remedies are available to
      holders of each?
   How is each regime evolving in the United States?
   Where are current legal developments taking us,
      and is it a place that makes sense?
   What's right and what's wrong with current pro-
      tection systems?
   How well will these protection systems apply to
      emerging technologies?

---

*Workshop held September 12-13, 1989, in Room GR 130, National Academy of Sciences,
2001 Wisconsin Avenue, N.W., Washington, D.C.

Opening remarks by Paul Goldstein

Panelists:
Pamela Samuelson     Emory School of Law
Donald Chisum        University of Washington
Robert Spinrad       Xerox Corporation

## 3. Software Protection From Various Vantage Points     11:00 a.m.

Mitchell Kapor, Organizer & Moderator

Questions:
Assessment of the environment for software
    from various perspectives:
        small companies
        large companies
        integrated companies
Is financial return to developers the only or the
    most effective incentive for getting good
    work done?
Where is the balance between the relative impor-
    tance of original prototype creation and the
    process of turning prototypes into products?
Does that have any ramifications for forms of
    protection?
What happens as commercial software standards
    begin to emerge?

Opening remarks by Mitchell Kapor

Panelists:
Esther Dyson         EDventure Holdings, Inc.
Nat Goldhaber        The Cole Gilburne Fund
Lee Keet             Vanguard Atlantic, Limited
Harry Reinstein      Aion Corporation

## 4. What's Special About Software?     1:45 p.m.

Anita Jones, Organizer & Moderator

A.  Case Studies
Questions:
    What was developed?
    What was the essence you wished to protect?
    What legal method was selected for that
        protection?

How well did it work? What were the benefits, problems with it?

Opening remarks by Anita Jones

Panelists:
Charles Geschke          Adobe Systems, Inc.
John Muskivitch          The MacNeal-Schwendler
                         Corporation
Norris van den Berg      IBM Corporation

B. Discussion                                    3:00 p.m.

Questions:
   What is the essence of software creation as an
      intellectual activity?
   Where is the effort in software?
   How is the art of writing software likely to
      change in the future?
   Are legal approaches relevant to technical realities?

Opening remarks by Anita Jones

Panelists:
Randall Davis            Massachusettes
                         Institute of Technology
Gideon Frieder          Syracuse University
Mitchell Kapor          ON Technology, Inc.

*Wednesday, September 13*

5. **Differences in Legal Systems Worldwide**        9:00 a.m.

   Paul Goldstein, Organizer & Moderator

   Questions:
      What are the differences and similarities in inter-
         national patent, copyright, and trade secret law?
      What are current issues affecting international pro-
         tection?
      What factors affect these differences and similarities?
      How do they affect us?

   Panelists:
   Dennis Karjala          Arizona State University
   Michael Keplinger       Patent & Trademark Office

## 6. Other Forces Affecting Software                    10:15 a.m.

Peter Schneider, Organizer & Moderator

Questions:
   What are the forces other than protection sys-
      tems that affect the creation and dissemina-
      tion of software?
   What role do government policies, market forces,
      etc., play?
   Are there barriers to dissemination of knowledge
      and disincentives to creativity?
   How should we deal with the problems of protec-
      tion vs. standardization and need for compat-
      ibility?
   How should we balance the rewards for innova-
      tion with the importance of universally
      adopted interfaces, languages, and other
      functions needing standardization?
   Can software interfaces be defined separately
      from other elements of software, and if so,
      should they be separately protectable?
   Can programming languages be defined separately
      from other elements of software, and if so,
      should they be separately protectable?

Opening remarks by Peter Schneider

Panelists:
Stanley Besen    The RAND Corporation
Ruann Ernst      Hewlett Packard
Ronald Laurie    Irell & Manella

## 7. Open Discussion and Summary Session          1:30 p.m.

Lewis Branscomb, Organizer & Moderator

Questions:
   Are the existing legal regimes satisfactory for the
      protection of software?
   Is there a case for a sui generis protection system
      for software?
   If so, what might be its characteristics?
   What might be the benefits/costs to such an approach?
   Should there be different systems for different types

of software (applications, systems, languages, tools, databases, and so on)?

Different approaches for different phases of work (conception, algorithms, code)?

Are there articulable ideas that might make a positive difference in the evolution of legal protection for software?

How can communication be improved between software developers and policymakers/judges/lawyers?

Panelists:

| | |
|---|---|
| Jerome Reichman | Vanderbilt University |
| Michael Remington | House Judiciary Committee |

Steering Committee:

| | |
|---|---|
| Lewis M. Branscomb | Harvard University |
| Paul Goldstein | Stanford Law School |
| Anita K. Jones | University of Virginia |
| Mitchell D. Kapor | On Technology, Inc. |
| Michael O. Rabin | Harvard University |
| Peter R. Schneider | IBM Corporation |

8. **Closing remarks by Lewis Branscomb**                        3:30 p.m.

## PARTICIPANTS

Henry Beck
Lord Day & Lord, Barret Smith

Mark Bello
Alexandria, Virginia

Stanley M. Besen
The RAND Corporation

Marjory S. Blumenthal
National Research Council

Lewis M. Branscomb (Chair)
Harvard University

Donald S. Chisum
University of Washington

Randall Davis
Massachusetts Institute of
  Technology

Esther Dyson
EDventure Holdings, Inc.

Ruann Ernst
Hewlett-Packard

Francis D. Fisher
Cambridge, Massachusetts

Gideon Frieder
Syracuse University

Charles Geschke
Adobe Systems Incorporated

Nat Goldhaber
The Cole Gilburne Fund

Paul Goldstein
Stanford Law School

Allen R. Grogan
Blanc Gilburne Williams & Johnston

C.K. Gunsalus
University of Illinois

Bertram Herzog
Center for Information Technology
  Integration

Anita K. Jones
University of Virginia

Brian Kahin
Cambridge, Massachusetts

Mitchell D. Kapor
ON Technology, Inc.

Dennis S. Karjala
Arizona State University

Ernest E. Keet
Vanguard Atlantic Ltd.

Michael S. Keplinger
U.S. Patent & Trademark Office

Ronald S. Laurie
Irell & Manella

L. Thorne McCarty
Rutgers University

John Muskivitch
The MacNeal-Schwendler Corporation

Susan H. Nycum
Baker & McKenzie

Michael O. Rabin
Harvard University

Jerome H. Reichman
Vanderbilt University

Harry C. Reinstein
Aion Corporation

Michael J. Remington
U.S. House of Representatives

Pamela Samuelson
Emory University School of Law

Peter R. Schneider
IBM Corporation

John F. Shoch
Asset Management Company

Robert Spinrad
Xerox Corporation

Norris van den Berg
IBM Corporation

# Appendix B
# Intellectual Property Issues in Software
# Forum Program and Participants*

## PROGRAM

*Thursday, November 30*

9:00 a.m. **Overview**
Lewis M. Branscomb, Chair, Forum Steering Committee,
John F. Kennedy School of Government, Harvard
University
Esther Dyson, EDventure Holdings, Inc.
Ronald Laurie, Irell & Manella

10:30 p.m. **The Public Interest**
Lewis M. Branscomb [Moderator], John F. Kennedy
School of Government, Harvard University
Francis D. Fisher
Anita Jones, Department of Computer Science, University of Virginia
John F. Shoch, Asset Management Company

12:00 p.m. **Luncheon and Presentation: "Entrepreneur's Perspectives"**
Daniel Bricklin, President, Software Garden, Inc.

1:30 p.m. **How Software Is Special**

---

*Forum held November 30 and December 1, 1989, in the Lecture Room, National
Academy of Sciences, 2101 Constitution Avenue, N.W., Washington, D.C.

Anita Jones [Moderator], Department of Computer
Science, University of Virginia
Randall Davis, Artificial Intelligence Laboratory,
Massachusetts Institute of Technology
Robert Spinrad, Corporate Strategy Office, Xerox
Corporation
Bruce Tognazzini, Ministry Ltd. to Human Interface,
Apple Computer, Inc.

3:30 p.m. **Legal Challenges**
Paul Goldstein [Moderator], Stanford School of Law,
Stanford University
Morton D. Goldberg, Schwab Goldberg Price & Dannay
Michael Keplinger, Office of Legislation and International
Affairs, U.S. Patent and Trademark Office
Jerome Reichman, School of Law, Vanderbilt Univer-
sity

5:30 p.m. **Reception in the Rotunda**

6:45 p.m. **Dinner and Keynote Address: "The Ecology of
Innovation"**
Mitchell D. Kapor, Chairman, ON Technology, Inc.

*Friday, December 1*

8:45 a.m. **Introduction**
Lewis M. Branscomb, Chair, Forum Steering Committee,
John F. Kennedy School of Government,
Harvard University

9:00 a.m. **"Intellectual Property in the Global Market Place"**
Howard Figueroa, Commercial and Industry Relations,
IBM Corporation

9:45 a.m. **Interfaces/Standards/Business Entry**
Peter Schneider [Moderator], IBM Corporation
Scott G. Davis, Digital Equipment Corporation
Frank Ingari, Lotus Development
Harry C. Reinstein, Aion Corporation

. 11:20 p.m. **Issues for the Future**
Lewis M. Branscomb [Moderator], John F. Kennedy
School of Government, Harvard University
Donald S. Chisum, School of Law, University of Wash-
ington

Ernest E. Keet, Vanguard Atlantic Ltd.
Pamela Samuelson, School of Law, Emory University
Peter Schneider, IBM Corporation

12:30 p.m.  **Summary**
Lewis M. Branscomb, Chair, Forum Steering Committee, John F. Kennedy School of Government, Harvard University
Paul Goldstein, School of Law, Stanford University
Anita Jones, Department of Computer Science, University of Virginia
Mitchell D. Kapor, ON Technology, Inc.
Michael O. Rabin, Aiken Computer Laboratory, Harvard University
Peter Schneider, IBM Corporation

## PARTICIPANTS

John Atwood
U.S. Customs Service

Donald M. Austin
U.S. Department of Energy

Henry Beck
Lord Day & Lord, Barret Smith

Mark Bello
Alexandria, Virginia

Kathleen C. Bernard
Cray Research, Incorporated

Fred Blosser
The Bureau of National Affairs, Inc.

Marjory S. Blumenthal
National Research Council

Lewis M. Branscomb (Chair)
Harvard University

Joseph W.B. Bredie
The World Bank

Dan Bricklin
Software Garden, Inc.

Charles N. Brownstein
National Science Foundation

James Burger
Apple Computer Inc.

Dianne Callan
Lotus Development Corporation

John Carson
George Washington University

Lynn Robert Carter
Carnegie Mellon University

Richard P. Case
IBM Corporation

Virginia Castor
The Pentagon

David W. Cheney
Council on Competitiveness

Bernard Chern
National Science Foundation

Y.T. Chien
National Science Foundation

Donald S. Chisum
University of Washington

Anthony L. Clapes
IBM Corporation

Frank W. Connolly
American University

Eileen D. Cooke
American Library Association

Richard P. Corben
Hewlett-Packard

Randall Davis
Massachusetts Institute of Technology

Scott G. Davis
Digital Equipment Corporation

Esther Dyson
EDventure Holdings, Inc.

Howard G. Figueroa
IBM Corporation

Francis D. Fisher
Cambridge, Massachusetts

Gideon Frieder
Syracuse University

Ian M. Friedland
National Research Council

Thomas F. Gannon
Digital Equipment Corporation

Steven W. Gilbert
EDUCOM

Martin A. Goetz
Goetz Associates

Morton David Goldberg
Schwab Goldberg Price & Dannay

Paul Goldstein
Stanford Law School

Jacques J. Gorlin
Washington, D.C.

Stephen Gould
Library of Congress

Allen R. Grogan
Blanc Gilburne Williams & Johnston

C.K. Gunsalus
University of Illinois

Auke Haagsma
Delegation of the Commission of the
   European Communities

Herb Hellerman
Amdahl Corporation

Karen Hersey
North Carolina State University

Bertram Herzog
Center for Information
   Technology Integration

Heidi Hijikata
U.S. Department of Commerce

John D. Holmfeld
U.S. House of Representatives

Frank Ingari
Lotus Development Corporation

Luanne James
ADAPSO

J. Jancin, Jr.
IBM Corporation

Douglas C. Jerger
ADAPSO

Anita K. Jones
University of Virginia

Brian Kahin
Cambridge, Massachusetts

Robert E. Kahn
Corporation for National Research
   Initiatives

Mitchell D. Kapor
ON Technology, Inc.

Dennis S. Karjala
Arizona State University

Ernest E. Keet
Vanguard Atlantic Ltd.

Michael S. Keplinger
U.S. Patent & Trademark Office

Marilyn J. Kretsinger
Library of Congress

Ronald S. Laurie
Irell & Manella

Bruce A. Lehman
Swidler & Berlin

Mark Lieberman
U.S. Department of Commerce

Jean Loup
Association of Research Libraries

Patrice Lyons
Haley, Bader & Potts

Steven Metalitz
Information Industry Association

Pat Mortenson
University of Georgia

John Muskivitch
The MacNeal-Schwendler Corporation

David B. Nelson
U.S. Department of Energy

Jeff Nuechterlein
U.S. Senate

Susan H. Nycum
Baker & McKenzie

Hans J. Oser
National Research Council

Ron Palenski
ADAPSO

Abraham Peled
IBM Corporation

Michael O. Rabin
Harvard University

Jerome H. Reichman
Vanderbilt University

Ron Reiling
Digital Equipment Corporation

Harry C. Reinstein
Aion Corporation

Michael J. Remington
U.S. House of Representatives

Carol A. Risher
Association of American Publishers

William C. Rolland
National Electrical Manufacturers
  Association

Laurence C. Rosenberg
National Science Foundation

William Ryan
AT&T Bell Laboratories

Pamela Samuelson
Emory University School of Law

Peter R. Schneider
IBM Corporation

Robert Schware
The World Bank

Mary Shaw
Carnegie Mellon University

John F. Shoch
Asset Management Company

E.A. Silva
Office of Naval Research

Eric H. Smith
International Intellectual Property Alliance

Oliver R. Smoot
Computer & Business Equipment
  Manufacturers Association (CBEMA)

Alfred Z. Spector
Transarc Corporation

Robert Spinrad
Xerox Corporation

August W. Steinhilber
National School Boards Association

Richard H. Stern
Washington, D.C.

Alfred D. Sumberg
American Association of
  University Professors

Charles P. Thacker
Digital Equipment Corporation

Bruce Tognazzini
Apple Computer, Inc.

Joseph F. Traub
Columbia University

Ingrid A. Voorhees
Computer & Business Equipment
  Manufacturers Association (CBEMA)

Ralph Wachter
Office of Naval Research

Allen B. Wagner
University of California at Berkeley

Robert M. White
Microelectronics and Computer
  Technology Corporation

Edith Wilson
Burson-Marsteller

James D. Wilson
U.S. House of Representatives

Joan D. Winston
U. S. Congress

Helen M. Wood
U.S. Department of Commerce